Woodworking Treasures

Handyman Club Library™

Handyman Club of America
Minneapolis, Minnesota

Woodworking Treasures

Printed in 2004.

CREDITS

Tom Carpenter
Creative Director

Mark Johanson
Book Products Development Manager
Handyman Club of America

Dan Cary
Senior Book Production Assistant

Chris Marshall
Editorial Coordinator

Kam Ghaffari, Chris Marshall
Writers

Marti Naughton
Series Design, Art Direction & Production

Kim Bailey
Photographer

Tom Deveny, Jon Hegge, John Nadeau
Project Builders

Steve Anderson
Production Assistant

Bruce Kieffer
Technical Illustrations

John Drigot, Bob Ginn, Mark Johanson, Bruce Kieffer
Project Designers

Dan Kennedy
Book Production Manager

ISBN 1-58159-029-6
© 1998 Handyman Club of America
4 5 6 7 8 9 / 09 08 07 06 05 04

Handyman Club of America
12301 Whitewater Drive
Minnetonka, Minnesota 55343
www.handymanclub.com

Contents

Teak Cocktail Table (20)

Display Cabinet (50)

Jewelry Box (116)

Backyard Bird Feeder (80)

Made-to-order Mailbox (134)

Butcher-block Wine Bar (72)

Mission-style Coat Tree (150)

Arts & Crafts Bookcase (10)

Country Spice Cabinet (108)

Night Stand (88)

Turned Table Lamp (98)

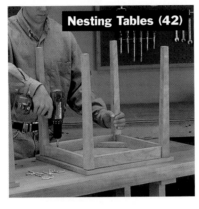
Nesting Tables (42)

Deluxe Tool Chest (28)

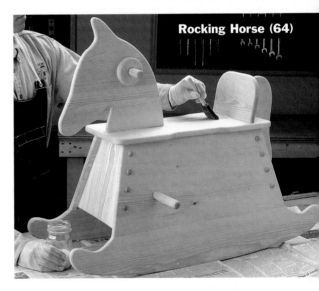
Rocking Horse (64)

Corner Cupboard (142)

Blanket Chest (124)

Introduction

Much of the satisfaction that comes with woodworking is in knowing that the projects we build may get passed on to future generations. In a way, we hope the end results of our efforts in the shop will tell a story about our craftsmanship that will continue beyond our years. Better still, family and friends likely will cherish our projects as one-of-a-kind treasures.

After poring over countless project designs, we've selected 16 of our favorites, which are compiled here in *Woodworking Treasures,* a new volume created exclusively for Members of the Handyman Club of America. Regardless of your experience level as a woodworker, you're sure to find many projects in this book that fit your present skill level and can be built with the tools you own today. You'll also find other projects that will challenge you to explore new techniques with different tools, increasing your capabilities as a woodworker.

Each project is presented with a complete cutting list, a shopping list, detailed plan drawings, beautiful color photographs of the project as it's being built, and straightforward step-by-step instructions to help you along. Take a bit of time to review the next few pages, which highlight some basic techniques that you'll find repeated throughout this book.

BUYING LUMBER

If you've never purchased hardwood at a traditional lumberyard before, learn the basics of buying wood. Knowing up-front how much (and what size) stock to buy for your project will save time, money and aggravation.

Unlike construction-grade lumber, hardwood and better-quality softwoods are sold by the *board foot.* A board foot is equal to one running (lineal) foot of a board that's 12 in. wide and 1 in. thick. To calculate precisely how many board feet of material you'll need for your project, multiply the length by the width by the thickness (expressed in inches) then divide that number by 144. You can make a quick and easy estimate by simply figuring out how many lineal feet of the stock you want to buy will equal one board foot.

But there's more to buying lumber than simply estimating board feet. Before you start a project, find out what dimensions your local supplier has the species available in and draw cutting diagrams for your project parts, as you would with plywood. Also, be aware that even lumber that's been planed on both sides at the mill will likely require additional planing, so you should buy wood that's at least ¼ in. thicker than the planned thickness of your project part. Hardwood is normally sold in random widths, so don't go to the lumberyard expecting to find a walnut 2 × 4.

1×6: 2 lineal ft. = 1 board ft.

2×6: 1 lineal ft. = 1 board ft.

4×4: 9 lineal in. = 1 board ft.

STEP 1: Run lumber through a thickness planer to create at least one smooth face. Flatten badly warped stock on a jointer first—planing won't flatten warps.

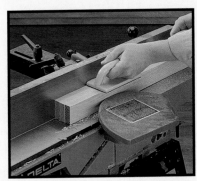

STEP 2: Plane one edge on a jointer until it's perfectly flat. Be sure that the jointer fence is square to the table and a planed face is against the jointer fence.

STEP 3: Rip the stock to width on the table saw. The jointed edge should ride against the saw fence with a planed face on the saw table. The stock is now square.

SQUARING STOCK

Flat, square lumber is essential to virtually all woodworking. Without it, joints cannot be drawn tightly together, workpieces won't line up and doors and drawers will not operate properly. To be square means that each face of a workpiece is at a right angle to adjacent faces. Squaring stock involves planing one or more faces of a board, then flattening an edge so it forms a right angle to the planed face. Some lumber comes factory-planed and square from the mill. If you buy your lumber rough-sawn, however, use the three-step process shown above to square your stock. Regardless of the initial shape of your lumber, be sure to check all stock for square with a try square before using it.

EDGE-GLUING

Woodworking projects often require solid-wood panels wider than the width of available single boards. You could opt to use a piece of plywood and wrap it with wood edge-banding, but it's relatively easy to glue edge-jointed boards into a solid-wood panel of just about any size you need.

Select boards of consistent grain pattern and color and flatten their edges on a jointer. Arrange them so that the growth rings alternate. You can then glue and clamp the boards without further joint support, or use joint alignment aids, such as biscuits, as we show at right.

STEP 1: Arrange edge-jointed boards into a panel and draw a "V" across all panel joints. Mark short reference lines every 8-10 in. for biscuits or dowels.

STEP 2: Cut biscuit slots or dowel joints at each reference line.

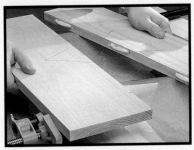

STEP 3: Apply glue to the biscuits or dowels and along one board edge. Press the boards together.

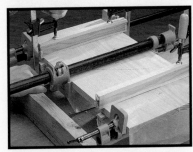

STEP 4: Clamp the panel together, alternating clamps above and below. Tighten clamps just enough to close the joints.

Featured Skill

MAKING BISCUIT JOINTS

Many of the projects in this book have parts that are assembled with biscuit joints. You'll see them used between solid boards in a glue-up panel to reinforce the glue joints as well as to align parts in cabinet and carcase construction. Biscuits are football-shaped disks made of compressed wood that come in several sizes. A biscuit joiner cuts semicircular slots in the mating parts of a joint. Because biscuits expand when they're exposed to wet glue, they lock the joint together. To make a biscuit joint, align the parts, mark the slot locations, cut the slots with the biscuit joiner, and glue the biscuits in place.

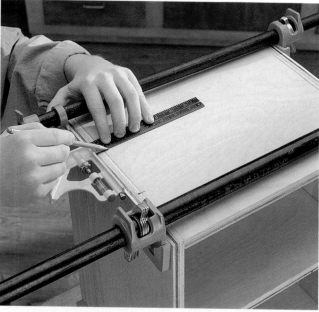

STEP 1: Dry-assemble and clamp the parts together. Draw straight lines across the joints to mark biscuit locations. Place biscuits at 6- to 8-in. intervals along each joint. Disassemble the parts.

STEP 2: Clamp each workpiece to the workbench and cut biscuit slots in the ends or edges, centering biscuit slots on the layout marks you made in Step 1.

STEP 3: Cut biscuit slots in the faces of workpieces to correspond with the slots you cut in Step 2. Clamp the flat edge of another workpiece in place to use as an alignment aid for the biscuit joiner base.

STEP 4: Dry-fit the parts together with biscuits in place. Then disassemble and spread glue along the mating parts of each joint and into the biscuit slots. Insert biscuits and assemble with clamps.

Featured Skill

APPLYING A WOOD FINISH

Fine wood finishing is a true art form. But fortunately, even if you don't have the time or interest to develop the art for yourself, today's wood finishing products allow even beginners to produce wood finishes that are more than satisfactory for most woodworking projects. If you're new to wood finishing, experiment with a few different finishing materials until you find a compatible combination of staining agent and topcoat material that you're comfortable with. Consult experts for their advice, and always sample a finish on scrapwood before you apply it to the actual project.

STEP 1: Sand all surfaces with progressively finer sandpaper (up to 180- or 220-grit for most hardwood). A random-orbit sander works well.

STEP 2: Wipe the surfaces with a tack cloth to remove dust and other debris. Do this no more than 30 minutes before applying the finish.

STEP 3: Apply wood stain (optional) with a staining cloth or a brush. Follow the manufacturer's directions for coverage.

STEP 4: Wipe away excess stain, then reapply if a darker tone is desired. Allow the stain to dry at least overnight before proceeding.

STEP 5: Apply a very thin coat of the clear topcoating product you prefer. The most common finishing mistake is applying overly heavy coats.

STEP 6: Sand the first coat lightly after it dries, using 400-grit sandpaper. Wipe clean, then apply more thin coats (at least three total).

Arts & Crafts Bookcase

The popular Arts and Crafts furniture style (similar to the Mission style) is reflected in this attractive oak bookcase. Simple yet elegant, it will blend into just about any room. And because it's made mostly of oak plywood, the cost is relatively low.

Vital Statistics: Arts & Crafts Bookcase

TYPE: Bookcase

OVERALL SIZE: 30W by 48H by 13D

MATERIAL: White oak, white oak plywood

JOINERY: Biscuit, dado, half-lap, miter, butt joints

CONSTRUCTION DETAILS:
- Decorative arched cutouts on the base
- Glass lite panels are flush-mounted in doors against half-lap muntins
- Decorative cabinet top features chamfered solid oak edging
- Exposed plywood edges on carcase are concealed with iron-on veneer edge tape

FINISHING OPTIONS: For a traditional Arts and Crafts finish, apply a dark wood stain such as medium or dark walnut, followed by a satin-finish topcoat (we used tung oil). For a more contemporary look, use lighter wood stain, or topcoat only.

Building time

PREPARING STOCK
2-3 hours

LAYOUT
2-3 hours

CUTTING PARTS
3-4 hours

ASSEMBLY
2-3 hours

FINISHING
1-2 hours

TOTAL: 10-15 hours

Tools you'll use

- Jointer
- Table saw
- Planer
- Router with piloted ⅛-in. rabbet bit, ½-in. straight bit, ¾-in. straight bit, ⅜-in. rabbet bit
- Jig saw, band saw or scroll saw
- Biscuit joiner
- Bar, pipe, C-clamps
- Miter saw (power or hand)
- Drill press
- Drill/driver
- Right-angle drilling guide
- ¾-in. Forstner bit

HANDYMAN Shopping list

- [ ] (1) ¾ in. × 4 ft. × 8 ft. white oak plywood (preferably quartersawn)
- [ ] (1) ¼ in. × 4 ft. × 4 ft. plywood for back panel (birch plywood)
- [ ] (5) 4/4 × 4 in. × 8 ft. white oak
- [ ] (6) 1⅜ × 2½ in. brass butt hinges
- [ ] (2) 1⅛ × 1⅛ in. wooden door pulls
- [ ] (20) Glass retainer pads
- [ ] Shelf support pins
- [ ] #6 × 1¼ in. flathead wood screws
- [ ] #20 biscuits
- [ ] ⅛-in. tempered glass (for door panels; cut to fit)
- [ ] Finishing materials

Arts & Crafts Bookcase

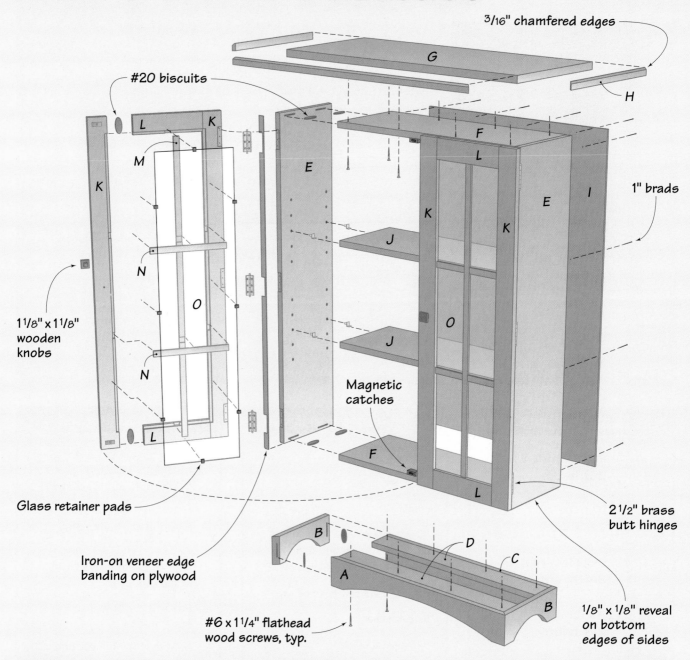

3/16" chamfered edges

#20 biscuits

1" brads

1 1/8" x 1 1/8" wooden knobs

Magnetic catches

Glass retainer pads

Iron-on veneer edge banding on plywood

2 1/2" brass butt hinges

#6 x 1 1/4" flathead wood screws, typ.

1/8" x 1/8" reveal on bottom edges of sides

Arts & Crafts Bookcase Cutting List

Part	No.	Size	Material
A. Base front	1	3/4 × 4 × 28 1/2 in.	White oak
B. Base sides	2	3/4 × 4 × 11 1/4 in.	"
C. Base back	1	3/4 × 4 × 27 in.	Scrap
D. Stretchers	2	3/4 × 3 × 27 in.	"
E. Sides	2	3/4 × 10 7/16 × 43 1/4 in.	Oak plywood
F. Top/bottom	2	3/4 × 10 7/16 × 27 in.	"
G. Cabinet top	1	3/4 × 12 3/4 × 29 1/2 in.	"
H. Edging	3	1/4 × 7/8 × *	White oak
I. Back	1	1/4 × 27 3/4 × 42 1/2 in.	Oak plywood
J. Shelves	2	3/4 × 9 7/8 × 26 3/4 in.	"
K. Stiles	4	3/4 × 2 1/2 × 43 in.	White oak
L. Rails	4	3/4 × 2 1/2 × 9 3/16 in.	"
M. Muntins (vert.)	2	1/4 × 3/4 × 38 3/4 in.	"
N. Muntins (hor.)	4	1/4 × 3/4 × 9 15/16 in.	"
O. Lites	2	1/8 × 9 7/8 × 38 11/16 in.	Glass

* Cut to fit

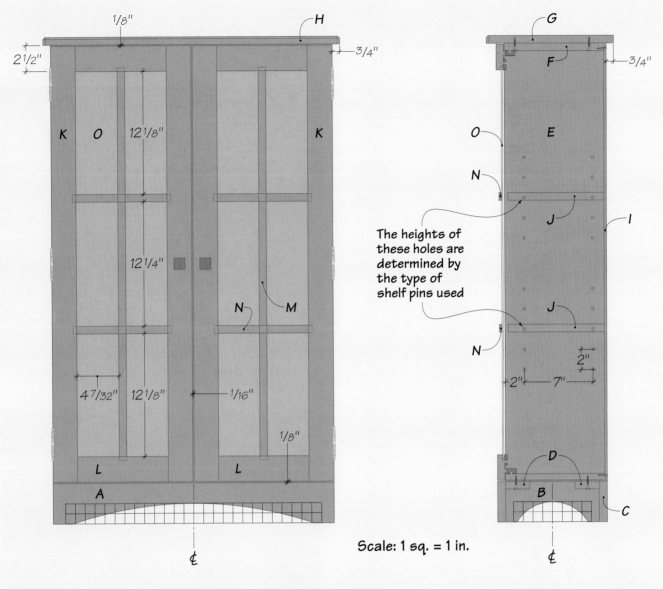

FRONT VIEW

SIDE SECTION VIEW

The heights of these holes are determined by the type of shelf pins used

Scale: 1 sq. = 1 in.

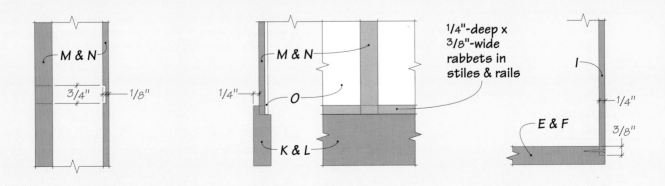

¹/₄"-deep x ³/₈"-wide rabbets in stiles & rails

MUNTIN HALF-LAP JOINTS

DOOR STILES & RAILS

RABBETS FOR BACK

PHOTO A: Apply iron-on veneer edge tape to the front edges of the sides, top, bottom and shelves.

MAKE THE CARCASE

The carcase for this bookcase is made with ¾-in. white oak plywood (if it's available and you're willing to spend a few extra dollars, use plywood with quartersawn white oak veneer). As with any plywood used for furnituremaking, you'll want to conceal the visible edges. To accomplish this, there are two options: you can attach thin strips of solid wood edging (as we do for the decorative cabinet top), or you can apply iron-on veneer edge strips.

1 Cut the carcase sides, top/bottom, shelves and cabinet top to size from ¾-in. oak plywood. To minimize splintering, use a fine-toothed plywood-cutting blade in your table saw.

2 Cut strips of iron-on veneer edge tape to cover the front edges of the sides, top/bottom, and shelves (we ordered a 50-ft. roll of 13⁄16-in.-thick white oak edge tape from a woodworkers' supply catalog). Use a pair of scissors to cut strips that are about an inch longer than the edge you're covering. There are special irons used to activate the adhesive backing on veneer edge tape, but an old household iron will work fine in most cases. We covered the face of the iron with foil to protect it from the adhesive and to distribute the heat a little more evenly. Turn the iron on to medium setting. Make sure the plywood edges are clean and free of debris, then clamp the workpiece panel in your bench vise, edge-up. Lay the strip of veneer tape along the edge (remove the protective backing strip, if it has one) and adjust it so the tape overhangs both the top and bottom edges. Touch the iron to the tape lightly in a few spots to tack it down. Then, starting at one end, hold the iron on the wood for a few seconds, covering as much surface area as possible. You'll see the adhesive start to melt. Remove the iron and immediately burnish the tape down to seat it, using a small wooden roller or a small block of

PHOTO B: Trim off the overhanging veneer edge tape so the tape is flush with the top and bottom of each workpiece. We used a hand trimmer with a blade that cuts flush to the panel.

wood. Work your way along the edge to the end of the panel **(See Photo A).**

3 When the veneer strip is bonded and the adhesive has cooled, trim the overhang flush to the panel faces and ends. We used a special veneer tape trimmer **(See Photo B).** If you're careful and use a straightedge, you can trim the excess with a utility knife or sharp chisel instead.

❹ Drill two rows of holes (front and back) in each side for the shelf support pins (**See Photo C**). Use a strip of perforated hardboard (Peg Board) cut to the panel width as a drilling template. Spacing the holes at every other pegboard hole should be adequate. Circle the desired holes on the template with a permanent marker before drilling, and clamp the template onto each side at the identical height from its bottom edge so the holes will be at the same level on both sides. Drill holes the correct size and depth for your shelf support pins. *TIP: If you've got a pretty good idea where you want the shelves to be, drill only two or three holes near the planned location for each shelf end—this will save time and avoid creating rows of unsightly holes on the cabinet interior.*

❺ Cut a ⅛ × ⅛-in. rabbet along the bottom, outer edge of each side panel. This will create a ⅛-in. reveal under the carcase to visually coincide with the ⅛-in. gap under the doors. We used a router and ⅛-in. piloted rabbeting bit to cut the rabbets.

❻ Cut biscuit slots at the joints between the sides, top and bottom to prepare them for assembly.

❼ Cut ⅜ × ¼-in. rabbets along the back inside edges of the top, bottom and sides to create a recess for the back panel (**See Photo D**).

❽ Dry-fit the carcase members, then finish-sand all the parts up to 150-grit. Use a light touch when sanding the veneer-taped edges to avoid sanding through.

❾ Glue the biscuit joints and clamp up the carcase (**See Photo**

PHOTO C: Drill holes for shelf-support pins in both sides, using a perforated hardboard drilling template and a right-angle drilling guide.

Rabbeting bit

PHOTO D: Cut a ¼ × ⅜-in. rabbet in the back edges of the top, bottom and sides to accommodate the back panel, using a router and a piloted ⅜-in. rabbeting bit (See inset photo).

E). Make sure to align the front edges of all the parts before applying clamping pressure. Measure the diagonals on the frame to make sure it's square, and adjust as needed. Use scrapwood clamping cauls to pad the clamp jaws and distribute pressure across the joints. Clean up any glue squeeze-out with a wet rag.

❿ Cut the back panel to size from ¼-in. plywood (we used inexpensive birch plywood because it can be stained to match just about any type of hardwood, including white oak). To keep the cabinet square, make sure the back is cut square and fits tightly in its rabbet. Finish-sand the interior face of the back, then install it in the carcase and secure it with 1-in. brads (do not use glue).

⓫ The decorative top panel that is attached to the carcase top is trimmed with solid oak edging before it's attached. Using your band saw or table saw to resaw thicker stock, cut about 60 lineal inches of ¼ × ⅞-in. white oak edging. Cut the pieces to length, miter the front corners and wrap them around the cabinet top. Glue the edging onto the front and sides of the panel, using clamps and full-length cauls. Try to install the edging so it's flush with the top surface of the cabinet top. If not, when the glue is dry you can flush up the edging to the plywood surfaces using a sharp hand plane or cabinet scraper.

⑫ Rout a ³⁄₁₆-in. chamfer at the top of the edging strips **(See Photo F)**. Finish-sand the cabinet top, and attach it to the carcase with #6 × 1¼-in. flathead wood screws, driven up through countersunk pilot holes in the underside of the carcase top. The cabinet top should overhang the carcase by ¾ in. on the sides and back.

MAKE THE DOORS

⑬ Cut the stiles and rails for the door frames to size from solid white oak. *TIP: To assure that the door parts will fit properly, careful jointing and planing of the stock is important. After jointing one face of the rough lumber flat, remove stock equally off both faces with the planer. Joint and plane it halfway down and let it sit overnight with narrow plywood strips, or stickers, in between the boards to allow air to flow all around them. Then, joint the stock flat again and plane it to final thickness. Be sure to joint one edge before rip-cutting the parts to width.*

⑭ Cut biscuit joints to join the rails to the stiles, and glue and clamp the door frames together **(See Photo G)**. Make sure the frames are absolutely square by measuring the diagonals and make corrections as necessary. When the glue is dry, unclamp the frames and smooth the joints with a scraper.

⑮ To create recesses for the glass lite panels, cut a ¼-in.-deep × ⅜-in.-wide rabbet around the inside edges of the door frames. Square off the corners of the recesses with a wood chisel.

PHOTO E: Assemble the carcase, using glue and biscuits. Measure across the diagonals to make sure the carcase is square, and adjust the clamps as necessary.

PHOTO F: Rout a ³⁄₁₆-in. chamfer around the front and side edges of the cabinet top.

PHOTO G: Clamp the door frames together, using glue and biscuited butt joints.

16 We added decorative wood strips (called muntins) to the door frames to create a multi-lite panel effect (a standard treatment with glass doors in Arts and Crafts designs). The muntins fit together with half-lap joints, with the ends set into small mortises in the glass-recess rabbets on the inside edges of the door frames. To cut the mortises, begin by marking centerpoints along the inside edges of the glass recess rabbets (See *Front View* on page 13 for spacing). We used a ¾-in. Forstner bit in the drill press to drill out the ¼-in.-deep mortises, then squared up the edges with a wood chisel **(See Photo H)**. A ½-in.-thick piece of scrap clamped next to the inside frame edge provides a drilling surface where the bit extends past the edge of the frame.

17 Resaw strips of white oak to ¼ in. thick and ¾ in. wide to make the muntins. A band saw is the safest tool for cutting small, thin workpieces like the muntin strips. Cross-cut the strips to fit inside the door frames.

18 The vertical and horizontal muntins are joined using half-lap joints. Lay out the joints, and cut the ⅛-in.-deep × ¾-in.-wide laps with a router and a ¾-in. straight bit **(See Photo I)**. Clamp the two verticals together and rout dadoes into the back faces of both at once. Clamp the four horizontals together and rout a dado through the center of all the front faces at once. Use a clamped-on straightedge to guide the cuts and a scrap backer board to prevent tearout.

19 Apply glue to the half-lap joints and clamp the muntins together, making sure the assemblies are square. Finish-sand both faces of the door frames and the muntins, then fit the muntin assemblies into the doors and glue and clamp them in place **(See Photo J)**.

CONSTRUCT THE BASE

20 Joint and plane white oak stock to ¾ in. thick, and rip-cut the base front and sides to 4 in. wide. Cut the parts to length, with 45° mitered ends for the front corner joints (the backs of the sides are square).

21 Draw the endpoints and tops of the arched cutouts on the base front and sides, using the grid pattern on page 13 as a guide. Place each workpiece facedown on a piece of scrap plywood. Tack a long finish nail into the plywood next to the wood at the marked points along its lower edge. Then, tack another nail into the workpiece, ⅛ in. down from the

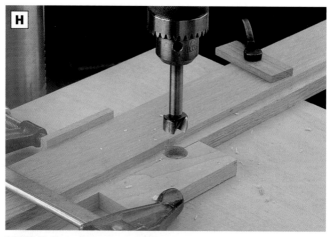

PHOTO H: Use a ¾-in. Forstner bit to remove the waste material from the ¼-in.-deep mortises for the ends of the muntins. A scrap board clamped to the workpiece provides a surface for the drill bit.

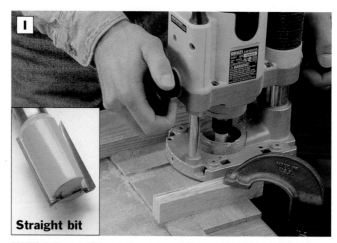

Straight bit

PHOTO I: Rout half-lap dadoes through the muntin strips, using a straightedge guide and a router with a ¾-in. straight bit. Gang the muntins together before routing.

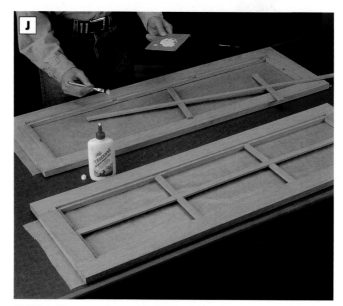

PHOTO J: Glue the muntin assemblies together, then glue the assemblies into the mortises in the door frames.

PHOTO K: Flex a piece of ⅛-in. tempered hardboard to create a smooth arc for tracing the cut profiles onto the base front and sides.

PHOTO L: Cut biscuit slots in the base parts. Adjust the biscuit joiner fence to 45° for the front mitered joints. The rear joints and the stretchers have straight 90° biscuited butt joints.

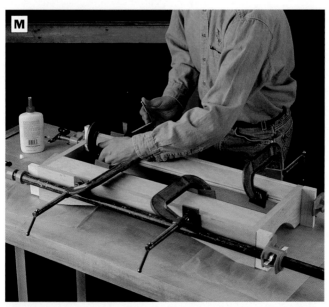

PHOTO M: Glue and clamp the base parts together. The mitered front joints should be clamped in both directions.

PHOTO N: Attach the base to the carcase by driving #6 × 1¼-in. flat-head wood screws up through the base stretchers and into the bottom of the carcase.

top mark. Cut a strip of ⅛-in.-thick tempered hardboard to 1 in. wide and about 32 in. long. Slip the strip over the top nail, with the ends behind the end-point nails so it bends evenly. Trace along the top edge to draw the cutout profiles in the workpieces **(See Photo K).**

❷❷ Cut the base back and the two stretchers to size from ¾-in. scrap hardwood or plywood. Cut slots for #20 biscuits at the joints between base parts **(See**

Photo L). Consult the exploded view diagram on page 12 for a view of how the base parts fit together.

❷❸ Dry-fit the base assembly and test to make sure it's flush with back and sides of the carcase, and extends ¾ in. past the front edge of the carcase. Adjust as needed, then glue and clamp the assembly together, reinforcing with #20 biscuits **(See Photo M).** When dry, make sure all the glue is removed and finish-sand the base.

HANG THE DOORS

24 Cut mortises for butt hinges in the door frames and carcase sides, using a sharp chisel. We used three 1⅜ × 2½-in. brass butt hinges per door. Install the hinges and hang the doors to make sure they open and close properly.

25 Remove the doors and hinges, then apply a wood finish to the project. We used dark walnut wood stain with three coats of tung oil for a traditional, dark Arts and Crafts finish. Be sure to finish-sand thoroughly and wipe all surfaces with a tack cloth before applying the finish. To prevent warping, finish the back of the bookcase the same way as the rest of the bookcase.

26 After the finish dries, attach the base assembly to the bottom of the bookcase carcase with #6 × 1¼-in. flathead wood screws **(See Photo N)**.

27 Install the glass lites in the door frames. We had two pieces of ⅛-in.-thick tempered glass cut to size at a local hardware store for the project. Tempered glass is less prone to breaking than ordinary window glass. But we waited until we'd finished and hung the door before ordering the glass, just in case the dimensions came out differently than those listed in the *Cutting List* on page 12. To install the glass, set each panel into a door frame recess, then install glass retainer pads behind the glass panels in the door frame to hold the panes in place **(See Photo O)**.

28 Drill holes through the inner door stiles for attaching the door pulls. We used 1⅛-in.-square wooden knobs.

PHOTO O: Secure the glass in the door frames with glass retainer pads that are screwed to the rails and stiles to hold the glass against the rabbets and the muntins. Use 10 pads per door.

PHOTO P: Screw the hinges into their mortises and hang the bookcase doors. Make sure they operate properly and adjust the hinges if necessary.

29 Reattach the doors, handling them with care to avoid breaking the glass **(See Photo P)**.

30 Install magnetic door catches at the top and bottom of the bookcase, following the manufacturer's instructions.

31 Install the shelf pins and insert the shelves at the desired height—they'll look best if they align with the horizontal muntins.

Teak Cocktail Table

Impress guests at your next patio or deck party when you set their refreshments on this handsome cocktail table. Our cocktail table is made of teak—a dense, highly weather-resistant hardwood used in better-quality wood boatbuilding. The tabletop features spaced slats to provide for good drainage, as well as exposed splines around the edges. The overall design could be modified for a full-sized picnic table.

Vital Statistics: Teak Cocktail Table

TYPE: Cocktail table

OVERALL SIZE: 18D tabletop by 18H

MATERIAL: Teak

JOINERY: Mortise-and-tenon joints, floating tenons

CONSTRUCTION DETAILS:

· Table is made of weather-resistant teak, with brass and stainless-steel hardware and waterproof polyurethane glue so it can be used outdoors

· Tabletop rails are joined with spline tenons into an octagon shape and then cut round

· Slat tenons are pinned in place rather than glued to allow for wood movement

FINISHING OPTIONS: Finish with teak oil if the table will be used indoors. The wood can be left unfinished if it will be an outdoor piece, and the teak will age to a silvery gray. Otherwise, topcoat with a quality outdoor wood preservative with UV protectant to preserve the natural wood tones

Building time

PREPARING STOCK
2-3 hours

LAYOUT
3-4 hours

CUTTING PARTS
2-3 hours

ASSEMBLY
2-4 hours

FINISHING
1-2 hours

TOTAL: 10-16 hours

Tools you'll use

· Planer

· Router table

· Router with piloted chamfer bit, V-groove bit, ¼-in. slot-cutting bit, ½-in. straight bit

· Power miter saw

· Band (strap) clamp

· Bar clamps

· Jig saw or band saw

· Table saw with tenon jig

· Drill press

· Drill/driver

· Wood chisels

Shopping list

☐ (1) ¾ × 6 in. × 8 ft. teak

☐ (1) 1½ × 1½ in. × 6 ft. teak

☐ (4) Brass "L" brackets, screws

☐ Polyurethane wood glue

☐ ½-in. stainless-steel brads

☐ Finishing materials

☐ Nylon glides

Teak Cocktail Table

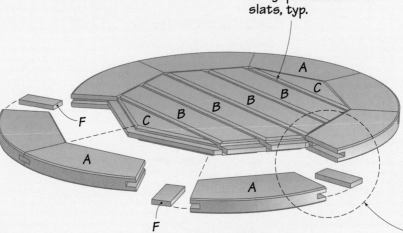

1/4" gaps between slats, typ.

A
C
B
B
B
B
B
C
F
A
A
F

See Detail: Table-top rails & slats

1 1/2" x 1 1/2" brass "L" brackets with #6 x 1/2" brass wood screws

E

E

See Detail: Mortise & tenon joints

1/8" chamfers on all exposed edges except bottoms of legs

D

D

Teak Cocktail Table Cutting List			
Part	**No.**	**Size**	**Material**
A. Top rails	8	$3/4 \times 3 1/4 \times 7 11/16$ in.	Teak
B. Inside slats	4	$3/4 \times 2 \times 14 1/2$ in.	"
C. Outside slats	2	$3/4 \times 2 1/2 \times 12$ in.	"
D. Legs	4	$1 1/2 \times 1 1/2 \times 17 1/4$ in.	"
E. Aprons	4	$3/4 \times 2 1/2 \times 10 1/4$ in.	"
F. Splines	8	$1/4 \times 1 \times 2 3/4$ in.	"

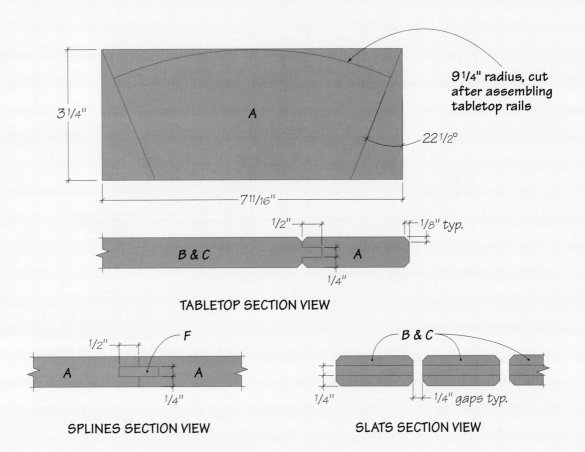

9¼" radius, cut
after assembling
tabletop rails

22½°

3¼"

A

7¹¹⁄₁₆"

1/2"

1/8" typ.

B & C

A

1/4"

TABLETOP SECTION VIEW

F

1/2"

A

A

1/4"

SPLINES SECTION VIEW

B & C

1/4"

1/4" gaps typ.

SLATS SECTION VIEW

DETAILS: TABLETOP RAILS & SLATS

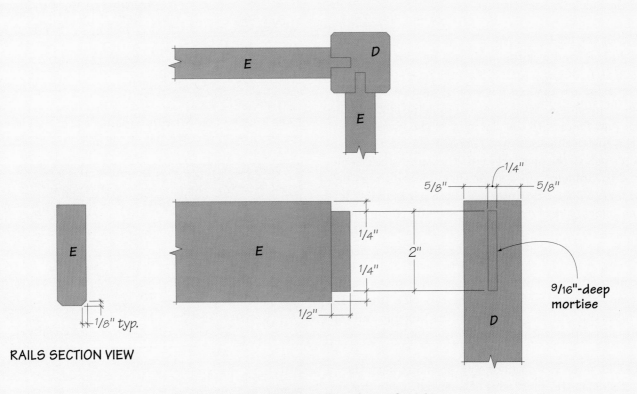

E

D

E

1/4"

5/8"

5/8"

E

1/4"

2"

1/4"

9/16"-deep
mortise

E

1/8" typ.

1/2"

D

RAILS SECTION VIEW

DETAIL: MORTISE & TENON JOINTS
(LEG TO RAIL)

MAKE THE TABLETOP RAIL ASSEMBLY

1 Surface plane your tabletop stock to ¾ in. thick and rip-cut to 3¼ in. wide. Rip enough teak stock to make all eight tabletop rails.

2 Install a chamfer bit in the router table and cut a ⅛-in. chamfer along the top and bottom of one long edge of the tabletop rail workpieces.

3 Install a ¼-in. piloted slot-cutting bit in the router table and set the bit height ¼ in. off the surface of the router table so the cutter will cut a centered ¼-in.-wide slot in the stock. Set the fence for a ½-in.-deep cut. Rout a slot along the chamfered edge of the stock **(See Photo A).**

4 Set the blade of a power miter saw 22½° to the right of 0° and lock the angle setting. Cut this angle on a strip of scrap lumber to serve as a stopblock and flip it against the saw fence so its angle is opposite the blade angle. Set a length of tabletop stock against the saw fence with the slot against the fence and trim the workpiece near the end. Then flip the table-top stock so the slot faces out. The scrap stock angle and the tabletop stock angle should now fit together to form a 45° angle. Interlock these parts and slide the tabletop stock/scrap block assembly along the saw fence until the blade will cut the tabletop stock piece at 7¹¹⁄₁₆, yielding a rail that's 7¹¹⁄₁₆ in. long on its edge with the slot on its narrow end. Fasten the stopblock to the saw table at this location (we used a screw) and cut the first tabletop rail **(See Photo B).** This setup will allow you to cut the tabletop rails one after the other without moving the stopblock.

5 Cut seven more rails, being careful to keep the slot side on the short edge of each rail. To do this, you'll need to flip the stock over, cut off the end angle and flip the stock back with each new rail you cut.

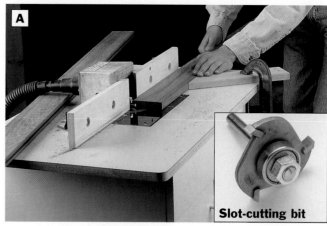

PHOTO A: With a slot-cutting bit (See inset photo) in the router table, rout a ¼-in.-wide × ½-in.-deep groove into the edge of the tabletop rail stock. Use a featherboard to hold the stock against the fence.

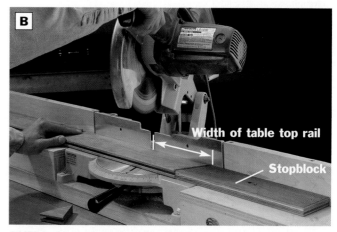

PHOTO B: Cut the tabletop rails to length with a 22½° angle on each end. Attach an angled stopblock to the saw table for consistent cuts.

PHOTO C: Rout spline grooves in the angled ends of the tabletop rails. Use a pushblock to aid in running the narrow pieces across the cutter and to back up the cut, preventing chipout.

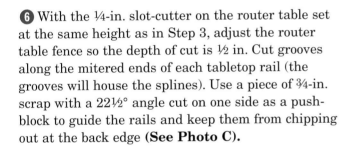

PHOTO D: Glue the splines into the tabletop rail end grooves. Wipe the mating parts first with mineral spirits to remove the natural oils in the wood. Spread the glue evenly with a glue brush. Wear latex gloves and have mineral spirits and a rag handy to wipe up squeeze-out.

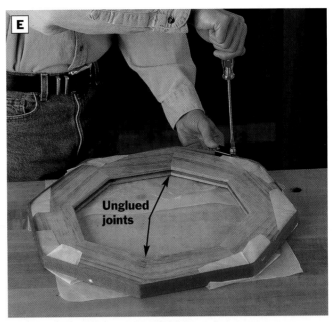

PHOTO E: Clamp the top rail assembly with a strap clamp, leaving two opposite joints unglued. Use wax paper around the glued corners to keep the strap from bonding to the wood.

6 With the ¼-in. slot-cutter on the router table set at the same height as in Step 3, adjust the router table fence so the depth of cut is ½ in. Cut grooves along the mitered ends of each tabletop rail (the grooves will house the splines). Use a piece of ¾-in. scrap with a 22½° angle cut on one side as a push-block to guide the rails and keep them from chipping out at the back edge **(See Photo C).**

7 Cut eight splines that are ¼ × 1 × 2¾ in. each. Then glue up the tabletop rails in two sections of four rails each. Wipe the mating surfaces with mineral spirits first, then apply polyurethane glue to the side grooves on each rail and insert the splines **(See Photo D).** The splines won't extend the full length of the joint, so align the splines flush with the bottom of the groove in the short side of each rail. NOTE: *Polyurethane glue cures by reacting with the moisture in the wood, so moisten the splines before assembling each joint.*

8 After the two rail sections are assembled, fit them together with two splines (don't use glue) and clamp the tabletop together tightly with a strap clamp **(See Photo E).** You'll glue the two tabletop sections together later. Slip wax paper between the corners and the clamp's strap to keep glue squeeze-out from gluing the clamp to the rails. Let the setup dry thoroughly, then remove the clamp.

PHOTO F: Insert ¼-in. spacers between the slats and clamp them together. Lay the rail assembly over the slats and trace the interior of the assembly onto the slats.

INSTALL THE SLATS

9 Rip stock to width for the 2-in. inside and 2½-in. outside tabletop slats and cross-cut them to length.

10 On a flat surface, lay out the slats edge-to-edge, with the outside slats at the ends. Insert ¼-in. spacers to get the gaps between the slats **(See Photo F).**

11 Measure out ½ in. beyond the traced lines on all slats to allow for the length of the slat tenons, and draw new cutting lines using a straightedge or marking gauge. Remove the clamps and cut the slats one at a time along the cutting lines.

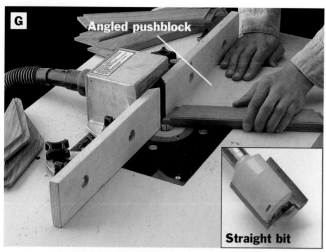

PHOTO G: Cut tenons into the angled ends of the slats with a ½-in. straight bit (See inset). Use an angled pushblock to guide the work.

Angled pushblock

Straight bit

PHOTO H: Rout ⅛-in. chamfers on the ends and edges of the slats using a V-groove bit in the router table. Use an angled pushblock to guide the workpiece.

PHOTO I: Glue and clamp the two halves of the tabletop rail assembly together with polyurethane glue and a strap clamp. Cover the glued corners with wax paper. Nail, rather than glue, the slats in place.

PHOTO J: Use a trammel to mark an 18-in.-dia. circle onto the underside of the tabletop, and cut it round with a band saw or jig saw.

⑫ Install a ½-in. straight bit in the router table. Set the bit height to ¼ in. Adjust the fence to cut ½-in.-long tenons on the ends each slat **(See Photo G).** NOTE: *Use a piece of angled scrap as a pushblock to guide the slats and keep the bit from tearing out the slat ends.* Dry-fit the slats into the top rail assembly, again inserting the ¼-in. spacers. Trim the slat tenons, as needed, to fit.

⑬ Disassemble the tabletop pieces and chamfer the edges and ends of all the slats and tabletop rails on the router table **(See Photo H).** We used a veining (V-groove) bit in the router table to cut the chamfers, and used the fence as a guide. Finish-sand all parts for the tabletop.

⑭ Reassemble the tabletop and glue the final two splined joints. Use a band clamp to secure the assem-

bly **(See Photo I).** Do not glue the slats. Instead, pin the joints through the center of each tenon by nailing one ½-in. stainless-steel brad up into each tenon. This will allow the slats to expand and contract with changes in temperature and humidity, especially if the table is kept outside. Let the glue dry.

⑮ Lay the tabletop facedown. Place a ¼-in. spacer snugly into the gap between the two center slats, and measure and mark the centerpoint of the tabletop assembly onto the spacer. Pin a piece of scrap to the spacer to serve as a trammel, and scribe an 18-in.-dia. circle around the centerpoint **(See Photo J).** Cut out the tabletop along this cutting line with a jig saw or a band saw. Sand the edge smooth, and use a piloted chamfer bit to rout a ⅛-in. chamfer around the top and bottom edge of the tabletop.

PHOTO K: Drill out the leg mortises on the drill press to ½-in. depth. Clean up the waste from the shoulder of the mortises with a chisel.

PHOTO L: Glue and clamp the legs and rails together. Use clamp pads between the clamp jaws and mineral spirits to clean up squeeze-out.

MAKE THE LEG ASSEMBLY

16 Rip- and cross-cut the four legs and four aprons to size.

17 Lay out two ¼-in.-wide mortises in the top of each leg, centering them on two adjacent sides. The mortises should be 2 in. long, starting ¼ in. down from the top ends (See *Detail: Mortise & Tenon Joints,* page 23). Cut the ½-in.-deep mortises by drilling side-by-side ¼-in.-dia. holes on the drill press, then clean and square up the mortises with a wood chisel to the layout lines **(See Photo K).**

18 Use a table saw and a tenon jig or router and straight bit to cut a ¼-in.-thick × ½-in.-deep × 2-in.-long tenon on each end of all four leg rails.

19 Rout a ⅛-in. chamfer on all edges of the table legs and the two lower edges of each leg apron. Finish-sand these parts.

20 Glue and assemble the legs and leg rails with the rail chamfers facing the leg bottoms using polyurethane glue and clamps **(See Photo L).** Use clamp pads between the clamp jaws and legs, to protect the wood.

FINISHING TOUCHES

21 Lay the tabletop facedown and set the leg assembly on top of it. Attach the leg rails to the underside of the top with four brass L-brackets and ½-in. brass or stainless-steel screws **(See Photo M).** Drill pilot holes for the screws first.

PHOTO M: Attach the tabletop to the rails and legs using brass L-brackets. Drill pilot holes before driving the screws.

22 Finish the table with teak oil if you plan to use the table indoors. If the table will be used outdoors, you can leave it unfinished to weather to a silvery gray or topcoat it with wood preservative with UV protectant to retain the color of the wood. The natural oils in teak will resist rot and insects. Attach nylon glides to the foot bottoms so the legs won't absorb water through their ends.

Deluxe Tool Chest

Every woodworker dreams of owning a first-class, handmade tool chest for storing and exhibiting his most cherished tools. Made from white oak and white oak plywood, with walnut accents, this handsome chest is a challenging project that you'll display with pride for years to come.

Vital Statistics: Deluxe Tool Chest

TYPE: Tool chest

OVERALL SIZE: 22W by 15H by 12D

MATERIAL: White oak, white oak plywood, walnut

JOINERY: Tongue-and-groove frame-and-panels, butt joints reinforced with screws, finger joints, dado joints

CONSTRUCTION DETAILS:
- Strong, decorative finger joints on drawers
- Walnut handles with cove-shaped finger pulls
- Drawers mount on wooden slides
- Makes efficient use of materials
- Upper compartment and three drawers for large tool-storage capacity

FINISHING OPTIONS: Clear, protective topcoat

Building time

PREPARING STOCK
3-4 hours

LAYOUT
4-6 hours

CUTTING PARTS
6-8 hours

ASSEMBLY
8-10 hours

FINISHING
1-2 hours

TOTAL: 22-30 hours

Tools you'll use

- Jointer
- Table saw
- Planer
- Router table with ¾-in. core box bit, straight bits (¼, ¾ in.), chamfer bit
- Bar or pipe clamps
- Jig saw
- Band saw
- Plug cutter
- Drill press
- Flush-cutting hand saw
- Compass
- Drill/driver
- Combination square

Shopping list

- ☐ (1) ¼ in. × 4 ft. × 4 ft. white oak plywood
- ☐ (2) ¾ × 8 in. × 8 ft. white oak
- ☐ (1) ¾ × 4 in. × 2 ft. white oak
- ☐ Walnut (scrap)
- ☐ 20⅜ in. brass piano hinge
- ☐ (2) Brass lid supports
- ☐ #8 brass flathead wood screws (1¼-, 2-in.)
- ☐ #8 × 1 in. flathead wood screws
- ☐ #6 × ½ in. brass screws
- ☐ Wood glue

Deluxe Tool Chest

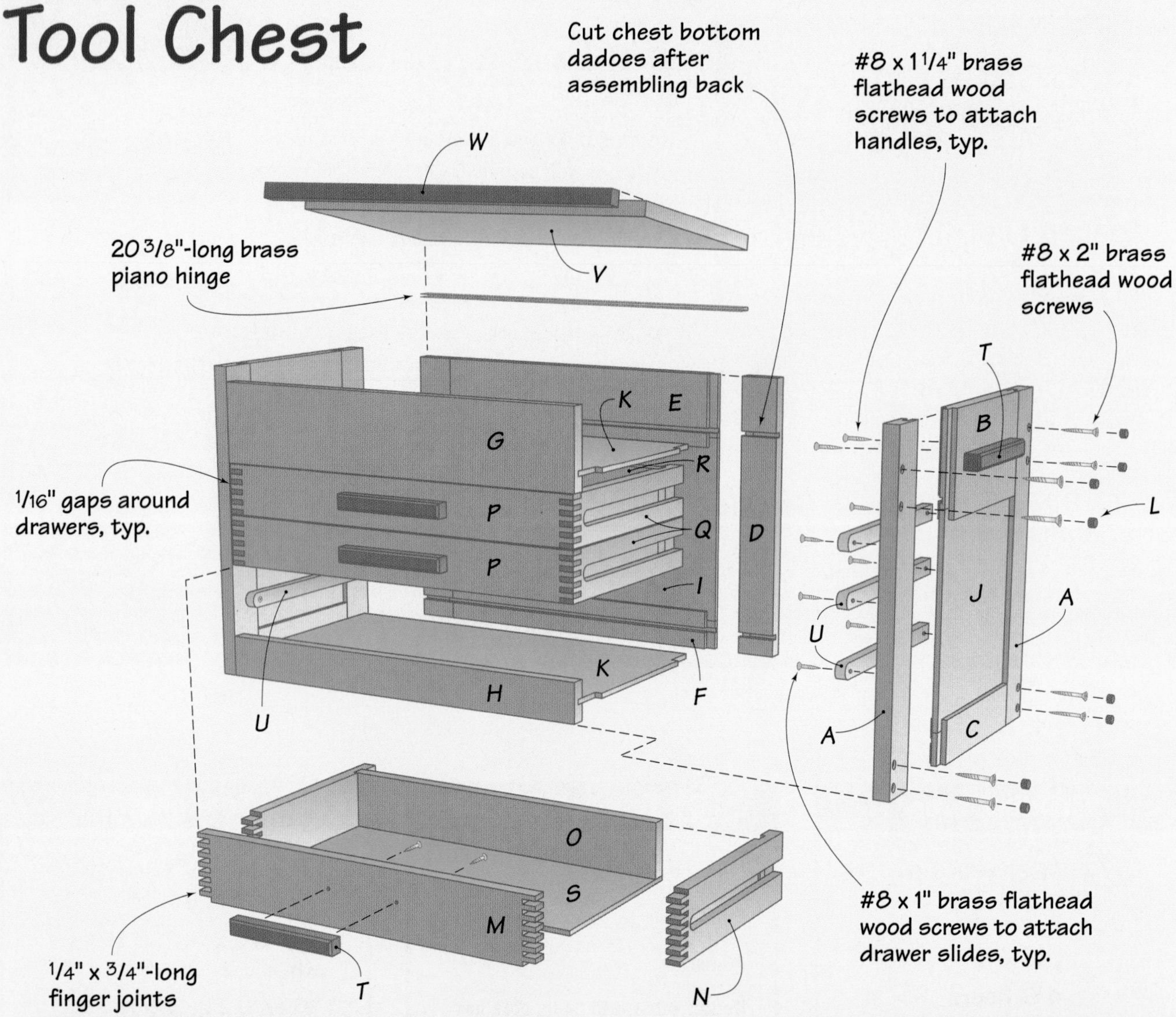

Cut chest bottom
dadoes after
assembling back

#8 x 1¼" brass
flathead wood
screws to attach
handles, typ.

#8 x 2" brass
flathead wood
screws

20 ³/8"-long brass
piano hinge

W

V

K   E

G

R

¹/16" gaps around
drawers, typ.

P

Q

P

T

B

L

D

I

J

A

H

K

U

F

A

C

A

U

#8 x 1" brass flathead
wood screws to attach
drawer slides, typ.

O

S

M

¼" x ³/4"-long
finger joints

T

N

Deluxe Tool Chest Cutting List							
Part	**No.**	**Size**	**Material**	**Part**	**No.**	**Size**	**Material**
A. Side stiles	4	¾ × 2 × 15½ in.	Oak	**M.** Drawer front (lg)	1	¾ × 3½ × 20⅜ in.	Oak
B. Side rails (top)	2	¾ × 4¾ × 9 in.	"	**N.** Drawer sides (lg)	2	¾ × 3½ × 11¼ in.	"
C. Side rails (btm)	2	¾ × 2 × 9 in.	"	**O.** Drawer back (lg)	1	¾ × 3 × 19⅜ in.	"
D. Back stiles	2	¾ × 2 × 14⁹/16 in.	"	**P.** Drawer fronts (sm)	2	¾ × 2½ × 20⅜ in.	"
E. Back rail (top)	1	¾ × 3¹³/16 × 17½ in.	"	**Q.** Drawer sides (sm)	4	¾ × 2½ × 11¼ in.	"
F. Back rail (btm)	1	¾ × 2 × 17½ in.	"	**R.** Drawer backs (sm)	2	¾ × 2 × 19⅜ in.	"
G. Front rail (top)	1	¾ × 4 × 20½ in.	"	**S.** Drawer bottoms	3	¼ × 9¾ × 19⅜ in.	Plywood
H. Front rail (btm)	1	¾ × 2 × 20½ in.	"	**T.** Handles	5	¾ × ¾ × 6 in.	Walnut
I. Back panel	1	¼ × 17½ × 9¾ in.	Plywood	**U.** Drawer slides	6	½ × ¾ × 10¼ in.	Oak
J. Side panels	2	¼ × 9¾ × 9 in.	"	**V.** Lid	1	¾ × 11½ × 20⅜ in.	"
K. Chest bottoms	2	¼ × 11¼ × 21¼ in.	"	**W.** Lid handle	1	¾ × ¾ × 20⅜ in.	Walnut
L. Screw plugs	16	⅜ dia. × ¼ in.	Walnut				

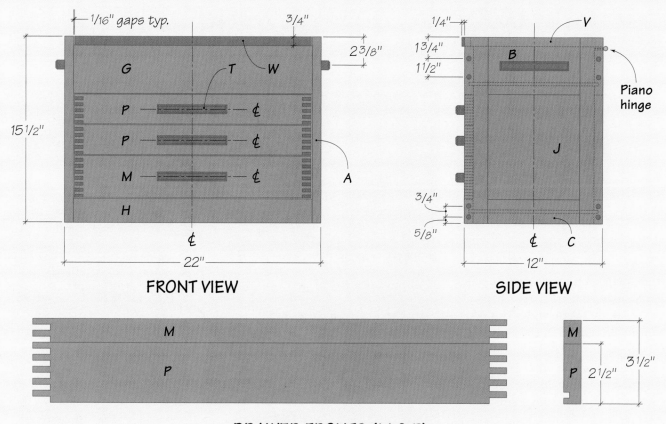

FRONT VIEW

1/16" gaps typ.

3/4"

2 3/8"

G T W

P ₵

P ₵

M ₵

H

15 1/2"

₵

22"

SIDE VIEW

1/4"

1 3/4"

1 1/2"

V

B

Piano hinge

J

3/4"

5/8"

₵ C

12"

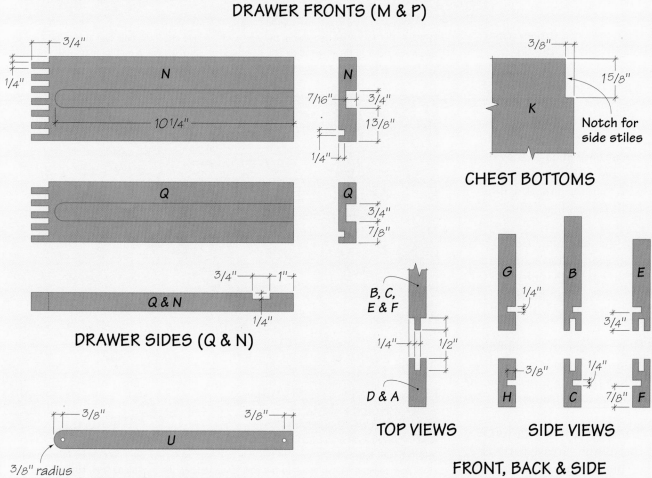

M

P

DRAWER FRONTS (M & P)

M

P

3 1/2"

2 1/2"

3/4"

1/4"

N

10 1/4"

N

7/16" 3/4"

1 3/8"

1/4"

3/8"

15/8"

K

Notch for side stiles

CHEST BOTTOMS

Q

Q

3/4"

7/8"

3/4" 1"

Q & N

1/4"

DRAWER SIDES (Q & N)

B, C, E & F

G B E

1/4"

3/4"

1/4" 1/2"

D & A

3/8"

H

3/8"

C

1/4"

7/8"

F

TOP VIEWS   **SIDE VIEWS**

3/8"

3/8"

U

3/8" radius

DRAWER SLIDES (U)

FRONT, BACK & SIDE STILES & RAILS (A-H)

MAKE THE LID

❶ The tool chest lid is edge-glued from strips of narrower white oak stock. Joint and rip three strips of ¾ in. oak to 3⅞ in. wide. The board that will be in the center of the glue-up will need to be jointed on both edges; the other two each only need jointing on one edge. Cross-cut the chest lid strips to 20⅝ in. long.

❷ Edge-glue the three strips together to create the lid.

❸ When the glue has dried, scrape, plane, and sand the lid panel flat and smooth. Joint one edge and rip it to 11½ in. wide. Cross-cut both ends so they're square, but only trim the lid to 20½ in. long for now. It will be cut to fit the cabinet later.

❹ Cut the lid handle from a piece of scrap walnut that's 20½ in. long. Rip-cut the handle to ¾ × ¾ in. (it will be cut to finished length later, along with the lid).

❺ Glue and clamp the lid handle to the front (jointed) edge of the lid. When the glue dries, sand the surfaces level and smooth.

BUILD THE SIDES & BACK

❻ Cut all the carcase parts to size. This includes the rails, stiles and insert panels for the frame-

PHOTO A: Cut ¼ × ½-in. grooves in the edges of the side and back rails and stiles. The grooves should be sized so the plywood panels fit into them snugly. Using a featherboard and pushstick, cut the grooves by making multiple passes with the table saw blade.

PHOTO B: Cut tenons in the ends of the side and back rails. Use the miter gauge to push the stock and clamp a spacer block to the saw fence to keep the workpiece from binding. The tenons are cut by removing ¼ in. of material from each side.

and-panel carcase sides, as well as the chest bottom panels that fit between the carcase sides, front and back.

7 Cut ¼-in.-wide × ½-in.-deep grooves for the panel inserts in the edges of the side and back stiles and rails. We used a dado-blade set installed in the table saw to cut the grooves **(See Photo A).**

8 Cut ¼-in.-thick × ½-in.-long tenons on the ends of the side and back rails. We used the dado-blade set for making these cuts, trimming ¼ in. off each side of the ¾-in.-thick rails and stiles. Use the miter gauge to give a square cut. To keep the workpieces from binding against the fence, clamp a reference spacer block to the fence and use it to set up your cuts **(See Photo B).**

9 Cut ¼-in.-wide × ⅜-in.-deep grooves for the chest bottoms into the edges of the side rails and both front rails **(See Photo C).** The chest bottoms should fit snugly into the grooves, so rather than using a dado-blade set, make two passes with a standard table saw blade to custom-fit the grooves to the actual thickness of the plywood used to make the chest bottoms (plywood is usually undersized from its nominal size). The grooves in the upper rails should be ¾ in. from the lower edge of each board (See *Side Views,* page 31). All the lower rails are the same width (2 in.) and should have their grooves cut ⅞ in. from the bottom edges, centered on the inside faces of the boards.

10 Finish-sand the rails, stiles and panels before assembly.

PHOTO C: Cut ¼ × ⅜-in. grooves for the upper and lower chest bottoms into the side and front rails. Use a featherboard and pushstick.

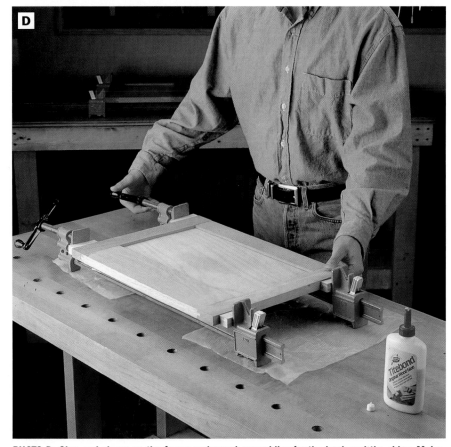

PHOTO D: Glue and clamp up the frame-and-panel assemblies for the back and the sides. Make sure the ends of the stiles are flush with the edges of the rails. Do not glue in the panels—they should "float" in the grooves.

PHOTO E: Using a jig saw, notch out the corners of the chest bottoms so they will fit around the ungrooved side stiles.

PHOTO F: Glue up the frame-and-panel assemblies and the chest bottoms to create the chest carcase. Reinforce the joints by driving screws through the side panels and into the ends of the front and back rails. Counterbore the pilot holes to accept ⅜-in.-dia. wood plugs.

⓫ Dry-assemble the sides and the back to test the fit. Trim a bit off the ends of the rail tenons if necessary so the joints come together tightly.

⓬ With the side and back panels inserted into the grooves (without glue), glue and clamp together the mortise-and-tenon joints at the stiles and rails **(See Photo D).**

ASSEMBLE THE CARCASE

⓭ Cut ¼-in.-deep × ⅜-in.-wide grooves for both the upper and lower chest bottoms in the assembled back frame. Cut all the way through, from end to end. Make the grooves the same distances from the bottom edge of the frame as those on the side frames, so they'll align when the carcase is assembled.

⓮ Cut ⅜-in.-wide × 1⅝-in.-deep notches in the corners of the chest bottoms, as shown in the detail illustration on page 31. The notches allow the bottoms to fit around the side stiles. Use a jig saw to cut the notches **(See Photo E).**

⓯ To assemble the carcase, lay the sides on a piece of scrap plywood, inside-face-down. Lay out and drill counterbored pilot holes for #8 × 1¼-in. wood screws through the side stiles. Center the holes on the locations for the ends of the front and back rails, two holes per joint.

⓰ Finish-sand all carcase parts (sides, back, front rails and carcase bottoms), and ease all sharp edges with 180-grit sandpaper.

⓱ Assemble the carcase with glue and #8 × 2 in. flathead wood screws **(See Photo F).** Attach the assembled sides to the front rails and the assembled back, with the chest bottoms glued into their grooves. Use padded clamps to hold the box together while you extend the pilot holes in the side stiles into the rail ends. The bottom edges of all the lower rails should be aligned. The top edge of the front rail should be ¾ in. lower than the tops of the sides, and the top edge of the back should be 15⁄16 in. lower than the tops of the sides.

18 Cut the screw plugs from walnut scrap, using a plug cutter mounted in your drill press **(See Photo G).** After making at least 16 plug cuts, resaw the walnut on a band saw to release the screw plugs **(See Photo H).**

19 Apply glue to the ends of the plugs and insert them into the counterbored screw holes, tapping each plug home with a mallet. When the glue is dry, trim the plugs flush to the surrounding wood surface with a flush-cutting saw or dovetail saw **(See Photo I).** Sand the plugs smooth.

MAKE THE DRAWERS
The drawer fronts and sides are joined with finger joints (also called box joints). Use a jig to make accurate finger joints (you can purchase a finger joint jig at most woodworking stores, or you can build your own, as we did). Always test the jig setup first by cutting joints in scrap wood of the same dimensions as the actual parts. The joints should fit together snugly, without requiring any pounding to assemble.

20 Cut the oak drawer parts to size. Cut the drawer backs about ¼ in. wider than specified in the *Cutting List* on page 30 (to about 2¼ and 3¼ in.).

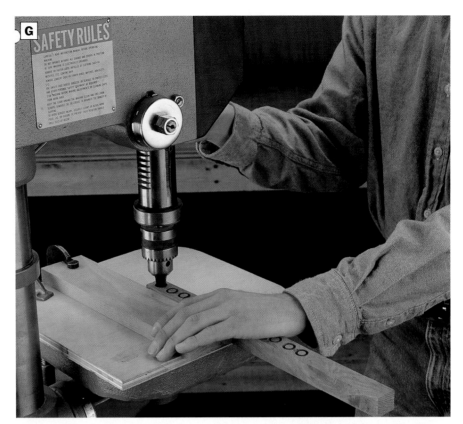

PHOTO G: Make walnut screw plugs on the drill press, using a ⅜-in. tapered plug cutter. Clamp a scrap piece to the drill press table to create a surface that helps keep the walnut stock stationary while you cut the plugs.

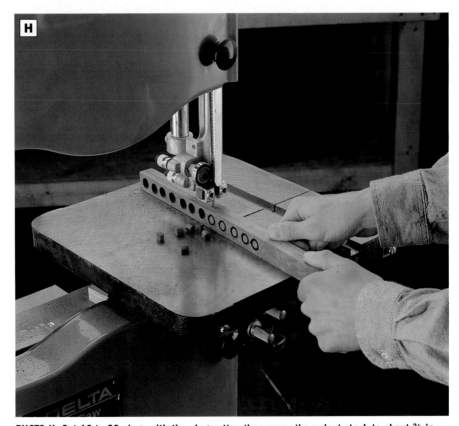

PHOTO H: Cut 16 to 20 plugs with the plug cutter, then resaw the walnut stock to about ⅜-in. thick to release the plugs.

to the fence for each cut. Shut off the saw and remove the workpiece after it clears the blades; don't drag it back through.

㉓ Reposition the workpiece so the slot you just cut fits down over the pin spacer, and make the next cut. Continue in this manner until all the joints in that end of the board are cut. Then flip it end-for-end and cut the fingers in the other end the same way. Make sure a pin is on the top.

㉔ Now, cut the mating joints in the front ends of the drawer sides. Since you started the joint with a pin on the first board, its mate must start with a slot (space). To do this, fit the first board you cut over the spacer strip, so the first pin will act as an offset spacer. Butt the mating board up against this board and cut a slot at the edge of the workpiece (**See Photo K**). Then remove the first board, move the mating piece over so the inside edge of the slot presses up against the spacer, and make the second cut. Continue to make cuts across the board, then cut the joint in the other drawer side by repeating the same procedure. Cut the finger joints for the other narrow drawer parts and then for the wider, lower drawer parts.

㉕ Rout $\frac{1}{4} \times \frac{1}{4}$-in. grooves for the drawer bottoms into the inside faces of the drawer sides and front, using a router with a $\frac{1}{4}$-in. straight bit (we used a router table, but you can use a router with a straightedge guide instead). The grooves should be stopped just before reaching the ends of the pins for the finger joints, but run all the way out the back ends of the drawer sides.

㉖ Trim the drawer backs to match the width of the other drawer parts, measured from the top edges down to the tops of the drawer bottom grooves.

㉗ The drawers will mount on wood glides attached to the inside faces of the chest sides. Grooves cut in the outer faces of the drawer sides fit over the glides.

PHOTO I: Use a flush-cutting saw or a dovetail saw to trim the walnut plugs flush. A flush-cutting saw has teeth without set so they won't damage the surrounding wood.

㉑ We built a jig and used a table saw with a dado-blade set to cut the finger joints used to join the drawer parts. To make the jig, clamp an auxiliary plywood fence, roughly 6 × 16 in., to the miter gauge. Cut a $\frac{1}{4}$-in.-wide × $\frac{3}{4}$-in.-deep slot about 6 in. from one end of the auxiliary fence by passing the fence over the dado-blade set. Cut a strip of hardwood to fit into the slot and serve as a pin spacer. Glue the spacer strip into the fence slot (you can see the spacer in place in *Photo J*). Now, reposition the auxiliary fence on the miter gauge so the inside face of the spacer is exactly $\frac{1}{4}$ in. (the thickness of one pin) from the saw blade.

㉒ Now you are ready to cut the finger joints. Start with the sides, front and backs for the narrower upper drawers. Stand the first workpiece (a drawer front) on end and butt its top edge up against the spacer strip and feed it over the blades (**See Photo J**). This will start the joint with a pin. When cutting, you can hold the board with your hand (hold it tightly, as the blades may tend to pull it) or clamp it

To cut the grooves in the drawer sides, install a ¾-in. straight bit in the router table and set the fence so the groove is the proper distance from the bottom edge of each board (this distance varies: See the *Drawer Sides* on page 31). Cut ¾-in.-wide × ⁷⁄₁₆-in.-deep grooves in several passes, taking off no more than ⅛ in. of material at a time, and stopping the cut 1 in. from the front edges of the workpieces **(See Photo L).**

28 Since they're not visible, the drawer backs are attached to the sides with ordinary dado joints. Cut the ¾-in.-wide × ¼-in.-deep dadoes 1 in. from the back edge of each side (see page 31) with the dado-blade set in the table saw **(See Photo M),** or with a router and ¾-in. straight bit.

29 Finish-sand the insides of the drawer parts, taking care not to distort the mating faces of the finger joints or to reduce the thickness at the ends of the drawer back pieces.

30 Assemble the drawers. Apply glue to the mating surfaces of the fingers with a small brush or thin glue stick. Clamp the finger joints in both directions and tighten the clamps just until the joints are tight **(See Photo N).** To ensure that the inside faces are bottomed out against the slot shoulders, special attention must be paid to the clamping blocks: You can off-set them from the joint altogether, as we did. Or, if you prefer direct pressure, you can cut notches in the clamping blocks so they only contact the side-grain fingers on each side of the joints. Clamp end-to-end across the backs, making sure the bottom edges of the back panels are flush with the tops of the drawer bottom grooves on the

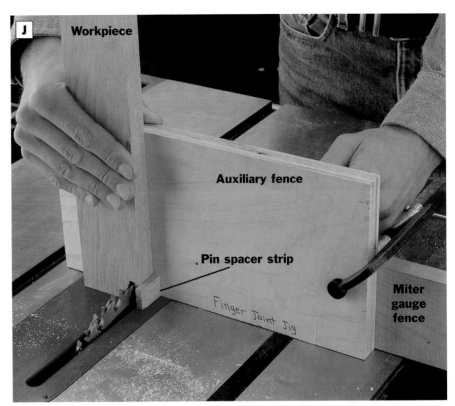

PHOTO J: The jig we used consists of an auxiliary fence clamped to the miter gauge fence. A ¼-in.-wide × ¾-in.-deep slot in the auxiliary fence is filled with a pin spacer strip to use as a gauge for aligning the finger joint cuts. Make the first finger joint cut with the workpiece butted against the pin spacer strip.

PHOTO K: For boards that start with a slot, not a pin, use the mating board as a guide for cutting the initial slot. The end slot on the cut board fits over the pin spacer strip, with the outer pin on the workpiece fitting between the strip and the saw blade.

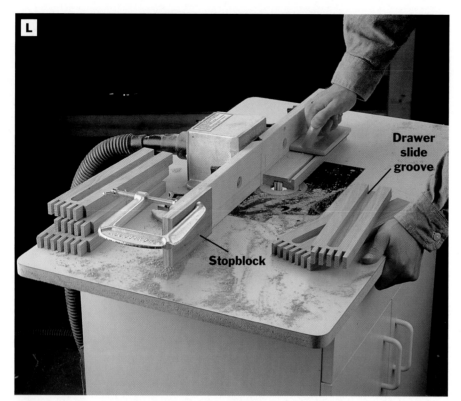

PHOTO L: After the drawer bottom grooves have been cut on the router table, rout grooves for the drawer slides. Both are stopped dadoes, cut in multiple passes.

Drawer slide groove

Stopblock

PHOTO M: Cut the drawer back dadoes on the table saw with a dado blade, miter gauge, and rip fence. Push the stock across the blades carefully to avoid binding the workpiece between the blades and the rip fence. Remove the stock after it has cleared the blades.

drawer sides (the drawer bottoms slip beneath the bottoms of the back panels and into the grooves in the sides and fronts). Measure the diagonals across the corners of the drawer boxes and adjust the clamps as necessary to assure the assemblies are square.

31 Cut the drawer bottoms to size from ¼-in. plywood, fitting them to the drawers. Make sure they are cut square.

32 Finish-sand the drawers and the bottoms, and ease all sharp edges with 180-grit sandpaper.

33 Slide one drawer bottom into its groove until it bottoms out in the drawer front and sits flush with the drawer back. It can be adjusted by tapping the bottom in at one end or the other or by clamping lightly across the corners. Then lock it in position by screwing the bottom in. With the drawer upside-down on a flat worksurface, drill evenly spaced, countersunk pilot holes through the bottom and into the drawer back and drive in three #8 × 1-in. screws (**See Photo O**). Do the same for the other two drawers.

MAKE & ATTACH THE HANDLES

34 Cut five ¾ × ¾ × 12-in. walnut strips for the handles. The finished length of the handles is 6 in., but the finger-pull coves are more easily and safely cut with the stock oversized.

35 Use a router table to rout the coves for the finger pulls on the undersides of the handles. Install a ¾-in.-dia. core box bit and adjust the cutter height and fence to cut the desired groove. Since the coves will be stopped at both ends, clamp startblocks and stopblocks to the fence to limit the cut. The cove should be 4½ in. long, leaving ¾ in. uncoved at each end of the final 6-in. length. To start the cut, push one end of a workpiece firmly against the startblock (on your right), keeping the other end on the table but away from the cutter. Holding the right end in the corner against the block, feed the other end into the cutter **(See Photo P)** until it rests against the fence. Then rout the cove by sliding the workpiece along the fence to the left until the other end strikes the stop-block **(See Photo Q).** Then, swing the trailing end away from the blade and remove the workpiece. Repeat the process with the other four handles.

36 Cut the handles to 6 in. long, making sure the coves are centered end-to-end.

37 Rout ¼-in. chamfers on all four outer edges of each handle Rout the long edges first. Then, rout the ends using a square scrap of ¾-in. plywood as a backup pushblock. Hold each handle tightly against the plywood and push the work-piece and the plywood block across the cutter together **(See Photo R).**

38 Finish-sand the handles, then attach them to the drawer fronts and the upper side rails, centered top-to-bottom and end-to-end. Use glue and two #8 × 1¼-in. wood screws per handle, driven through countersunk pilot holes and into the handles.

HANG THE DRAWERS

39 Make up the wooden drawer slides according to the dimensions given in the *Cutting List.* Trim the widths so they fit easily into the grooves of the drawer sides. The front end of each slide needs

PHOTO N: Glue up the drawers, offsetting the cauls to allow the finger joints to close tightly. Clamp the finger joints from both directions, and measure the diagonals from corner to corner to check for squareness.

PHOTO O: Slide the drawer bottoms into the grooves in the drawer sides and front. Secure the drawer bottoms with three screws driven through the drawer bottom and into the bottom edge of the drawer back. Do not use glue.

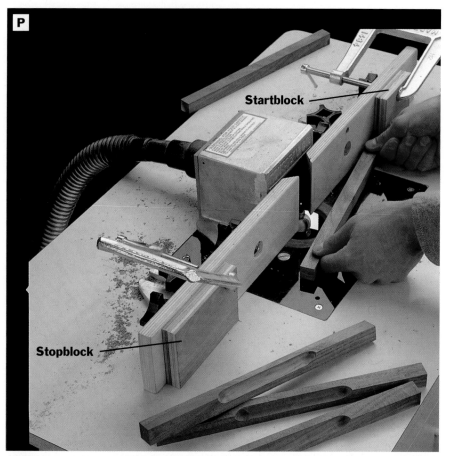

Startblock

Stopblock

PHOTO P: Rout cove-shaped finger pulls into the undersides of the handles using a router table fitted with a ¾-in. core box bit. Clamp a startblock and a stopblock to the table fence to guide your cuts.

to be rounded to a ⅜-in. radius. First, find the centerpoint of the circle by using the 45° end of a combination square to draw diagonals from the square corners. The point where these lines meet is the center and will also be where the screw holes will be located (do the same at the other end to locate the rear screw). Set a compass to ⅜-in. radius and swing an arc from this point around the end of the stock. Cut off the corners on a band saw and sand to the line with a stationary belt or disc sander, or cut to the line with a coping saw and file or sand smooth. Repeat this for all the drawer slides.

40 Mount the drawer slides, using spacers to align the heights. The bottom edges of the lower slides are 2⁵⁄₁₆ in. up from the chest bottom. The middle slides are 5⅜ in. up, and the upper slides are 7¹⁵⁄₁₆ in. up. Cut spacers from wood

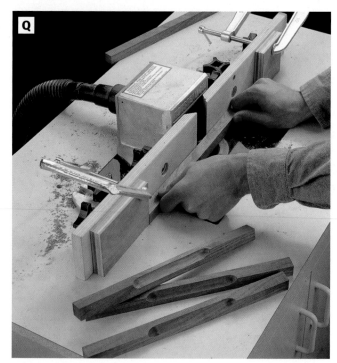

PHOTO Q: With the bit spinning, feed the workpiece up against the fence, making sure it contacts the startblock. Then, feed it toward the stopblock until the cut is finished.

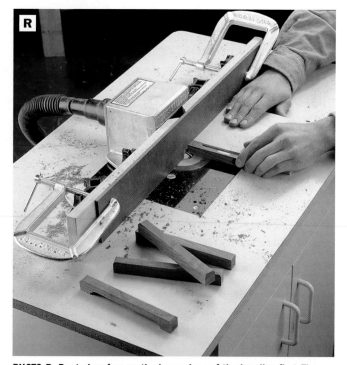

PHOTO R: Rout chamfers on the long edges of the handles first. Then use a backup pushblock to cut the chamfers into the ends of the handles (on the front faces of the handles only).

scrap and place them in between the drawer slides on the insides of the chest. Drill countersunk pilot holes in the slides at the marked points on the ends and screw the slides to the side stiles. Remove the spacers (**See Photo S).** After you attach the slides, check the fit of the drawers. You may need to trim the thickness of the slides a bit. There should be an even ⅟16-in. gap around the drawers.

FINISHING TOUCHES

41 Mount the lid. Attach the piano hinge to the lid and back temporarily with one screw at each end and one near the middle. Check the fit of the lid. Trim it so there is an even ⅟16-in. gap on both sides and the front edge has an even overhang. Once you're sure it's correct, mark the screw hole locations, remove the hinge and drive pilot holes for #6 × ½-in. brass wood screws. Drill pilot holes and drive screws along the length of the hinge (**See Photo T).**

42 Inspect the entire chest and smooth any roughness or sharp edges with sandpaper.

43 Prepare to apply the finish. Tape off the contact surfaces of the drawer slides and slide grooves to protect them from the finishing materials. Apply the finish (we used three coats of tung oil). When the finish has dried, remove the masking tape and wax the unfinished surfaces.

44 Attach the lid to the chest with the piano hinge.

45 Add brass lid supports on each side of the lid (optional).

PHOTO S: Mount the drawer slides using spacers to maintain even placement. After the slides are in place, remove the spacers.

PHOTO T: Dry-fit the lid by attaching the piano hinge with one or two screws in each end and another in the middle. Remove the hinge, once you're satisfied that everything fits together, and reattach it after the finish is applied.

Nesting Tables

Store three tables in the space you need for one by building these nesting tables. Our cherrywood tables are sized appropriately to fit beside sofas and chairs or could be the perfect display stands for plants or pottery. Set your table trio in the family room and they'll be at the ready for your next gameboard tournament.

Vital Statistics: Nesting Tables

TYPE: Nesting tables

OVERALL SIZE: Large: 24W by 24D by 24H

Medium: 19W by 19D by 20¾H

Small: 14W by 14D by 17½H

MATERIAL: Cherry, cherry plywood

JOINERY: Dowel, miter and butt joints

CONSTRUCTION DETAILS:
· Plywood tabletops with solid-wood edging
· Legs taper on two sides
· Dowel joints between the legs and aprons
· Tabletops secure with simple corner blocks

FINISHING OPTIONS: Danish oil; topcoat with three coats of satin polyurethane varnish if your tables will be subject to moisture

Building time

PREPARING STOCK
1-2 hours

LAYOUT
2-3 hours

CUTTING PARTS
2-3 hours

ASSEMBLY
2-3 hours

FINISHING
3-4 hours

TOTAL: 10-15 hours

Tools you'll use

· Jointer
· Table saw
· Random-orbit sander
· Drill/driver
· Tapering jig
· Doweling jig
· Japanese-style pull saw or fine-toothed back saw
· Bar or pipe clamps
· C-clamps

Shopping list

☐ (1) ¾ in. × 4 ft. × 4 ft. cherry plywood

☐ (3) 8/4 × 8/4 in. × 8 ft. cherry

☐ (1) ¾ × 8 in. × 8 ft. cherry

☐ (1) ⅜ in. × 6 ft. hardwood dowel

☐ #8 × 1¼ in. panhead wood screws

☐ Wood glue

☐ Finishing materials

Nesting Tables

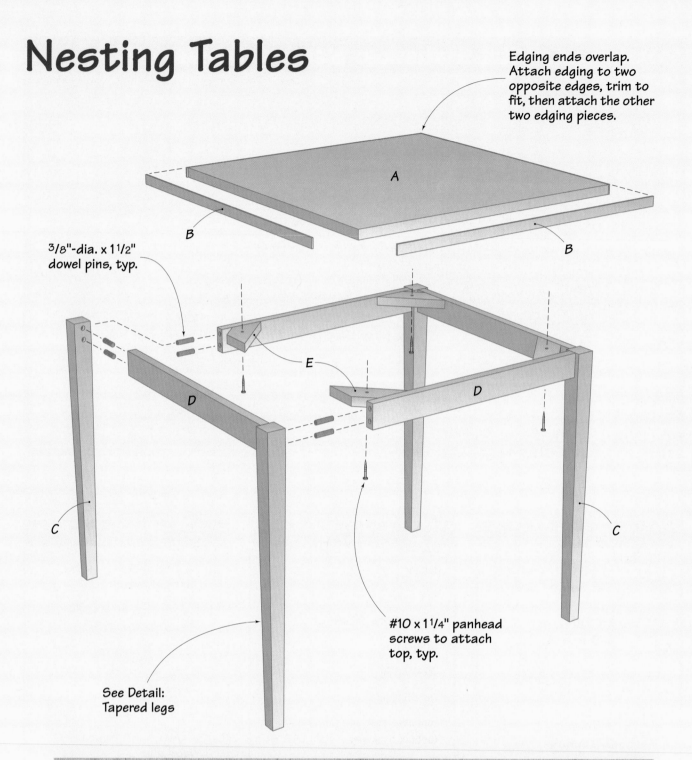

Edging ends overlap. Attach edging to two opposite edges, trim to fit, then attach the other two edging pieces.

A

B

B

³/8"-dia. x 1¹/2" dowel pins, typ.

E

D

D

C

C

#10 x 1¹/4" panhead screws to attach top, typ.

See Detail: Tapered legs

Nesting Tables Cutting List

Part	No.	Size (Large)	Size (Medium)	Size (Small)	Material
A. Top	1	³/4 × 23³/4 × 23³/4 in.	³/4 × 18³/4 × 18³/4 in.	³/4 × 13³/4 × 13³/4 in.	Cherry plywood
B. Edging	4	¹/8 × ¹³/16 × *	¹/8 × ¹³/16 × *	¹/8 × ¹³/16 × *	Cherry
C. Legs	4	1¹/2 × 1¹/2 × 23¹/4 in.	1¹/2 × 1¹/2 × 20 in.	1¹/2 × 1¹/2 × 16³/4 in.	"
D. Aprons	4	³/4 × 2 × 20 in.	³/4 × 2 × 15 in.	³/4 × 2 × 10 in.	"
E. Corner blocks	4	³/4 × 2 × 6 in.	³/4 × 2 × 6 in.	³/4 × 2 × 6 in.	"

Part quantities are given for one table only.   * Cut to fit

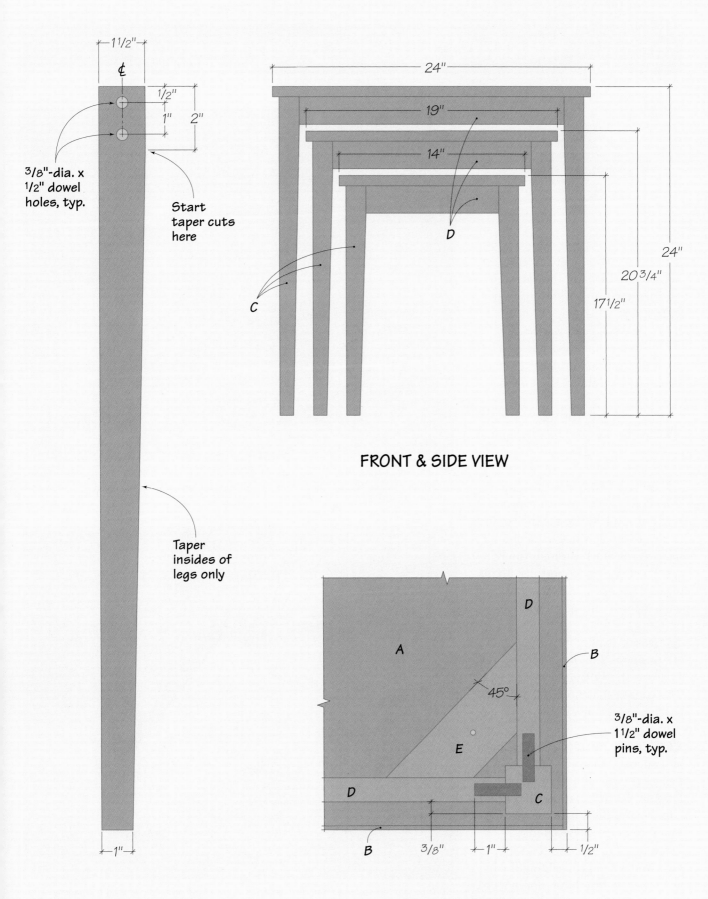

1 1/2"

℄

1/2"

1"

2"

3/8"-dia. x 1/2" dowel holes, typ.

Start taper cuts here

Taper insides of legs only

1"

24"

19"

14"

D

C

24"

20 3/4"

17 1/2"

FRONT & SIDE VIEW

D

A

B

45°

E

3/8"-dia. x 1 1/2" dowel pins, typ.

D

C

B

3/8"

1"

1/2"

DETAIL: TAPERED LEGS

SECTION VIEW: CORNER OF TOP

The construction steps to assemble these tables are the same for all three; the only differences are in the part sizes. Depending on how you work best, you could either build the tables one at a time, as separate projects, or mass-produce them all at once.

MAKE THE TOP

1 Cut the plywood tabletop panel to size.

2 Cut the four 1/8-in.-thick tabletop edging strips to size. Select a piece of solid cherry for the edging at least 13/16 in. thick. Run one edge of the stock through the jointer. Then rip-cut 1/8-in.-thick strips on the band saw with the jointed edge against the saw fence.

3 Cross-cut the four edging strips about 2 in. longer than listed in the *Cutting List,* page 44. The edging strips conceal the laminations and voids in the plywood.

4 Glue edging strips to two opposite edges of the tabletop. Select a face of the tabletop that will become the top, and position the edging so it lines up with the bottom face of the plywood and extends slightly above the top face. You'll sand the edging flush with the top face later. Spread glue evenly along both mating surfaces of the joints, and use

PHOTO A: Glue edging strips to two opposite sides of the plywood tabletop panel, using electrical tape to hold the strips in place. Tape the edging near the center of the panel first, then work outward toward the ends.

PHOTO B: Trim the excess edging flush with the edges of the plywood. We used a Japanese-style saw, but any fine-tooth hand saw will also work. Clamp the workpiece to your workbench to hold the panel steady as you cut.

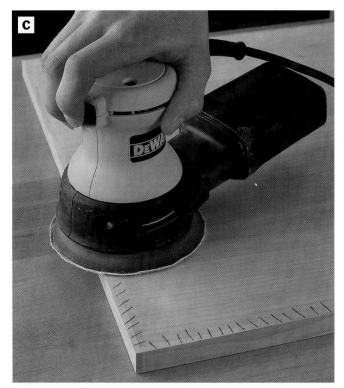

Tapering jig

PHOTO C: Sand the tabletop edging so it's flush with the plywood top. Draw short pencil marks across the top of the edging, then sand just until the pencil marks disappear.

PHOTO D: Cut the leg tapers—we used a tapering jig on the table saw. Cut tapers on two adjacent edges of each leg. Guide the workpiece with a pushstick.

strips of electrical tape spaced about 4 in. apart to "clamp" the edging strips onto the plywood (**See Photo A**). Let the glue dry and remove the tape.

5 Trim the overhanging ends of the attached edging strips flush with the exposed edges of the plywood (**See Photo B**). Use a fine-tooth back saw or hand saw (we used a Japanese-style saw). Then flush the overhangs with a few strokes of a small hand plane.

6 Attach the remaining two edging strips to the other two uncovered edges of the plywood so their ends overhang the edging already glued in place. When the glue dries, remove the tape and trim the overhanging ends of the edging flush.

7 Sand the top edges of the edging flush with the tabletop. To keep from oversanding, draw pencil marks across the edging and sand the edging just until the pencil lines disappear (**See Photo C**).

CUT THE LEG TAPERS

8 Cut the legs to length from stock that's at least 1½ in. square. Joint the edges of the legs flat.

9 Lay out tapers along two adjacent edges of each leg. The tapers start 2 in. down from the top of the

leg and extend to the bottom of the leg, reducing it to 1 in. square (**See Photo D**). We used a table saw with an adjustable tapering jig to make the leg tapers. For more information on using a tapering jig, see below. Sand the tapered edges smooth.

CUTTING TAPERS WITH A TAPERING JIG

Draw the desired taper on the work-piece and set the workpiece in the jig with the jig against the saw fence. Adjust the jig angle and the saw fence until the blade will follow the layout taper line. Lock the jig angle. Then push the jig along the fence, keeping the workpiece held tightly against the jig, to cut the taper. Guide the workpiece with a pushstick.

PHOTO E: Drill holes for the dowel joints between the aprons and legs. We used a doweling jig. For best results, drill the holes in the aprons first. Wrap masking tape around your drill bit to mark the hole depth. Drill dowel holes in all the aprons, then mark and drill the leg holes.

PHOTO F: Glue and clamp the apron together. Start by gluing and clamping a rail between pairs of legs. Once these glued-up assemblies dry, finish the apron by gluing the remaining two rails to the leg assemblies, inserting dowels into the joints.

MAKE THE TABLE BASE

10 Rip- and cross-cut the aprons to size, according to the dimensions given in the *Cutting List,* page 44, and sand them smooth.

11 The legs are joined to the aprons with dowel joints. For accuracy, we used a purchased doweling jig that allows you to clamp the jig to the workpiece and drill perfectly perpendicular holes. Lay out and drill ⅜-in.-dia. dowel holes in the legs and aprons using a doweling jig **(See Photo E).** Drill the dowel holes in the aprons first. Center the holes on the thickness of the aprons (See *Detail: Tapered Legs,* page 45, for hole placement). Drill two ½-in.-deep holes in the ends of each apron.

12 Drill pairs of 1-in.-deep dowel holes in the legs near the tops on the edges with the tapers to correspond with the holes you drilled in the aprons. The holes in the legs should be 1 in. deep.

13 Cut hardwood doweling to connect the legs to the aprons. Chamfer the ends of each dowel by rubbing the dowel edges off with sandpaper. Chamfered ends will make inserting the dowels into the leg and apron holes easier during glue-up.

14 Join the legs to the aprons. First, glue two legs to an apron, inserting dowels into the dowel holes. Clamp up the leg/apron assembly, using scrapwood pads between the clamp jaws to keep from marring the workpieces. Then glue up and clamp the other two legs to another apron in the same fashion. Let both apron assemblies dry and remove the clamps.

15 Glue and clamp the two leg/apron assemblies to the two remaining aprons, inserting dowels into the dowel holes **(See Photo F).** Check the resulting base assembly for square by measuring diagonally between the inside corners of each leg. Adjust the clamps until the diagonal measurements are equal to square the base assembly.

ATTACH THE TABLETOP

16 Cut four corner blocks from a length of 2-in.-wide maple stock, miter-cutting the ends of each corner block at 45° (See *Section View: Corner of Top* on page 45, for proper miter orientation). The corner blocks will provide a way to fasten the tabletop to the base with screws.

17 Drill a ⅛-in.-dia. pilot hole through each corner block. Center the hole across the width and length of each corner block. You'll attach the tabletop to the apron with screws through these holes later. Spread glue along the mitered edges of the corner blocks and position the blocks in the corners of the table base, flush with the top of the assembly. Clamp the blocks in place. NOTE: *You may need to create notched clamp pads to fit over the outer corner of each leg, in order to clamp the corner blocks in place. Otherwise, clamp the corner blocks with clamps that are outfitted with soft pads on the jaws to keep the jaws from marring the legs.*

⓲ Finish-sand the tabletop and the base assembly, then apply the finish of your choice. We used Danish oil and topcoated with three coats of polyurethane varnish **(See Photo G).** *TIP: When you finish the tabletop, slip spacer blocks underneath the workpiece to keep the finish from bonding with the drop cloth or newspaper underneath.* Finish both faces of the tabletop, as well as the edges and all surfaces of the base.

⓳ Fasten the tabletop to the base. Lay the tabletop facedown on your workbench and position the base on it so the tabletop overhangs the apron evenly on all sides. Drill pilot holes into the tabletop for #8 × 1¼-in. panhead screws, using the corner block holes as references. NOTE: *Wrap a strip of masking tape around your drill bit first and use it as a depth stop to keep from drilling all the way through the tabletop.* Drive the screws **(See Photo H).**

PHOTO G: Apply the finish to the tabletop and the base before attaching the two. We used Danish oil and topcoated with three coats of polyurethane varnish.

PHOTO H: Attach the tabletop to the base by screwing through the four corner blocks with #8 × 1¼-in. panhead wood screws.

Display Cabinet

Show off a variety of collectibles or family treasures in less space than it takes to store a vacuum cleaner with this display cabinet. Made of rich mahogany and accented with cabriole-style legs, decorative fluting, glass shelves and a mirrored back, this cabinet has enough sophisticated features to charm even the most discriminating of guests. It's sure to become a focal point of room decor.

Vital Statistics: Display Cabinet

TYPE: Display cabinet

OVERALL SIZE: 18W by 15½D by 60H

MATERIAL: Mahogany and birch plywood

JOINERY: Dowel, biscuit, butt, miter joints

CONSTRUCTION DETAILS:
· Fluted front stiles and profiled top edge add a sophisticated touch
· Shaped legs and a separate base give cabinet an elegant, traditional look
· Mirrored back, adjustable glass shelves and glass panels
· Glass panels held in place with wood stops

FINISHING OPTIONS: Wood stain and clear topcoat

Building time

PREPARING STOCK
3-4 hours

LAYOUT
4-6 hours

CUTTING PARTS
3-5 hours

ASSEMBLY
6-8 hours

FINISHING
2-3 hours

TOTAL: 18-26 hours

Tools you'll use

· Jointer
· Planer
· Table saw
· Power miter saw
· Band saw
· Hot glue gun
· Drill/driver
· Doweling jig
· Right-angle drilling guide
· Bar or pipe clamps
· Spring or C-clamps
· Plunge router with ¼-in. core box bit, ⅜-in. piloted rabbet bit, Roman ogee bit
· Biscuit joiner

Shopping list

☐ (4) ¾ × 6 in. × 8 ft. mahogany

☐ (1) ¾ in. × 1 ft. × 2 ft. birch plywood

☐ (1) ¼ in. × 2 ft. × 4 ft. birch plywood

☐ (1) ¼-in.-thick mirrored glass

☐ (1) ¼-in.-thick glass for shelves

☐ (1) ⅛-in.-thick glass for light panels

☐ ⅜-in.-dia. dowel

☐ #20 biscuits

☐ #8 × 1¼ in. flathead wood screws; ¾ in. brads

☐ (3) 3-in. brass ball-tip hinges; brass doorknob

☐ Shelf pins, bullet catch

☐ Glue, finishing materials

Display Cabinet

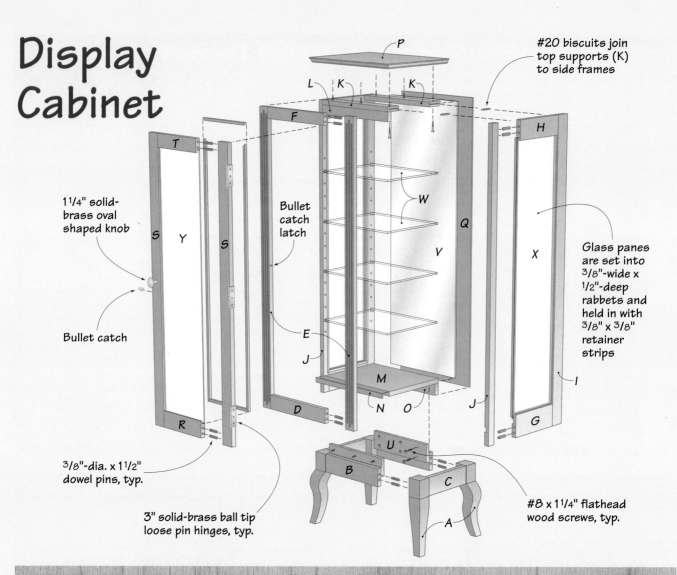

1¼" solid-brass oval shaped knob

Bullet catch

Bullet catch latch

³⁄₈"-dia. x 1½" dowel pins, typ.

3" solid-brass ball tip loose pin hinges, typ.

#20 biscuits join top supports (K) to side frames

Glass panes are set into ³⁄₈"-wide x ½"-deep rabbets and held in with ³⁄₈" x ³⁄₈" retainer strips

#8 x 1¼" flathead wood screws, typ.

Display Cabinet Cutting List

Part	No.	Size	Material	Part	No.	Size	Material
A. Legs	4	3 × 3 × 12 in.	Mahogany	**L.** Door stop	1	¾ × 1½ × 14½ in.	Mahogany
B. Base rails (front)	2	¾ × 3 × 12 in.	"	**M.** Bottom	1	¾ × 11¾ × 15 in.	Birch plywood
C. Base rails (side)	2	¾ × 3 × 9 in.	"	**N.** Bottom front edge	1	¼ × ¾ × 15 in.	Mahogany
D. Face frame lower rail	1	¾ × 2¼ × 12½ in.	"	**O.** Bottom back support	1	¾ × 2 × 14½ in.	"
E. Face frame stiles	2	¾ × 1¾ × 47¼ in.	"	**P.** Top	1	¾ × 14 × 17½ in.	"
F. Face frame upper rail	1	¾ × 1¾ × 12½ in.	"	**Q.** Back	1	¼ × 15¼ × 47¼ in.	Birch Plywood
G. Side frame lower rails	2	¾ × 3½ × 9 in.	"	**R.** Door rail (lower)	1	¾ × 2½ × 8⅜ in.	Mahogany
H. Side frame upper rails	2	¾ × 3 × 9 in.	"	**S.** Door stiles	2	¾ × 2 × 43⅛ in.	"
I. Side frame back stiles	2	¾ × 2¼ × 47¼ in.	"	**T.** Door rail (upper)	1	¾ × 2 × 8½ in.	"
J. Side frame front stiles	2	¾ × 1¼ × 47¼ in.	"	**U.** Base cleats	2	¾ × 3 × 12 in.	"
K. Top supports	2	¾ × 2½ × 14½ in.	"	**V.** Mirror	1	¼ × 14⁷⁄₁₆ × 44⅞ in.	Mirrored glass
				W. Shelves	4	¼ × 11⅞ × 14¼ in.	Glass
				X. Side panes	2	⅛ × 9⅝ × 41⅜ in.	"
				Y. Door pane	1	⅛ × 9⅛ × 39⅜ in.	"

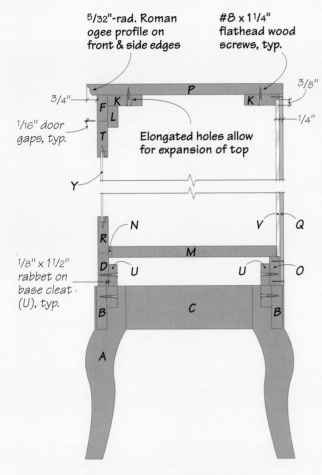

5/32"-rad. Roman ogee profile on front & side edges

#8 x 1 1/4" flathead wood screws, typ.

3/8"

3/4"

1/16" door gaps, typ.

Elongated holes allow for expansion of top

1/4"

P

F K

L

T

Y

N

V Q

R

M

D U U O

1/8" x 1 1/2" rabbet on base cleat (U), typ.

B

C

B

A

SIDE SECTION VIEW

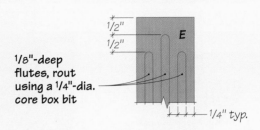

1/2"

1/2"

E

1/8"-deep flutes, rout using a 1/4"-dia. core box bit

1/4" typ.

FACE FRAME STILE FLUTING

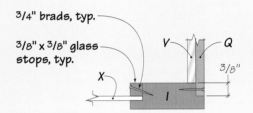

3/4" brads, typ.

3/8" x 3/8" glass stops, typ.

V Q

3/8"

X

I

REAR CORNER SECTION VIEW

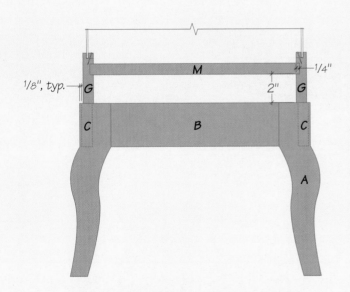

M

1/4"

1/8", typ. G

2"

G

C

B

C

A

LOWER FRONT SECTION VIEW

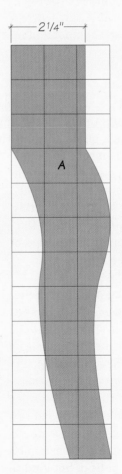

2 1/4"

A

Grid squares are 1" x 1"

ASSEMBLE THE BASE

❶ Laminate strips of mahogany to create a face-glued blank that's at least 3½ in. square and 50 in. long. After the glue cures, run one edge through your jointer until it's flat and smooth. Then, rip-cut the workpiece to 3⅛ in. square, making sure the jointed edge rides against your table saw fence. Cross-cut four 12-in.-long blanks for the legs.

❷ Draw the leg profile on a scrap piece of hardboard to create a leg template, using the grid drawing on page 53 as a guide. Cut out the template and smooth the edges with sandpaper. Trace the template shape onto two adjacent faces of each leg blank, butting the inside squared edge of the template against the corners of the wood (See Photo A).

❸ Cut out the profile of the legs on the band saw. This will need to be done in two stages. First cut along the outlines on one face of each blank (See Photo B). Try to cut each curved line in one smooth pass (this will be easier to do with a narrower band saw blade; we used a ¼-in.-wide blade). Reattach the waste pieces with several dabs of hot glue so the blank resumes its original shape (See Photo C).

PHOTO A: Create a leg template from scrap hardboard. Trace the leg shape onto one face of each leg blank, holding it flush against the inside top corner of the wood. Then trace the leg profile onto the adjacent side of the blank.

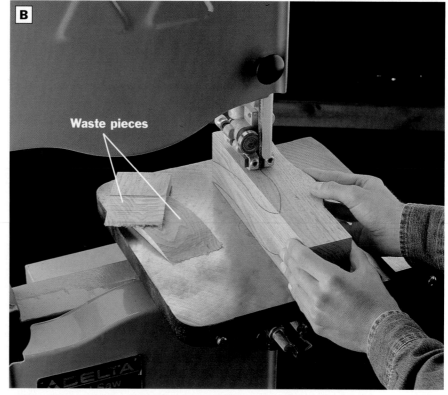

PHOTO B: To cut the legs to shape, start by cutting out the profile on one face of each leg blank on the band saw. Save the waste pieces, and try to cut them out in single sections.

4 Cut along the outlines of the adjacent edges **(See Photo D).** After these cuts are made, pop off the hot-glued waste pieces with a stiff putty knife and sand the sawn edges smooth. Cut and sand the profiles in all four leg blanks.

5 Cut the front and side base rails to size. The rails will attach to the legs with dowels. To prepare these dowel joints, first lay out and drill two ⅜-in.-dia. × ¾-in.-deep dowel holes in the ends of each rail using a doweling jig. Center the holes on the thickness of each rail and space them ¾ in. in from each edge.

6 Lay out and drill pairs of ⅜-in.-dia. × ¾-in.-deep dowel holes in the top edges of each leg to correspond with the holes you drilled in the rails. Drill these holes into the two adjacent edges of the legs that will face into the center of the base assembly. Position the holes so the rails will be ¼ in. back from the front surfaces of the legs when the base is assembled.

7 Finish-sand the base rails and the legs, and ease all sharp edges. Then, glue 1½-in.-long dowels into the dowel holes, spread glue on the ends of the rails and clamp up the base assembly with bar or pipe clamps **(See Photo E).**

8 Cut the base cleats to size, then rip-cut a ⅛-in.-deep by 1½-in.-wide rabbet along one face of each cleat on the table saw. The rabbet will create a ⅛-in. reveal between the cabinet and the base rails. Run the cleats on-edge through the blade, using an auxiliary fence attached to your table saw fence to support the workpieces and a featherboard and pushstick to guide them.

PHOTO C: Use a few dabs of hot glue to reattach the waste pieces to the leg blanks in their original positions.

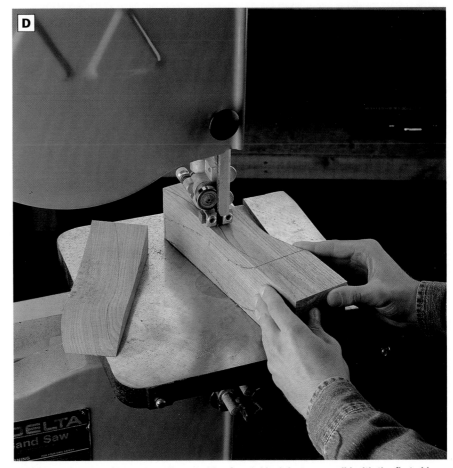

PHOTO D: Cut the profile on the adjacent side of each blank just as you did with the first side. The reattached waste pieces lend you flat surfaces for easier, accurate cuts.

PHOTO E: Glue the dowel joints, insert the dowels and assemble the base. Clamp across the sides with bar or pipe clamps. Measure across the corners of the assembly and square it up.

PHOTO F: Hold the base cleats in position with spring clamps so each cleat's rabbet shoulder is flush with the top of the adjoining front or back rail. Drill pilot holes and drive #8 × 1¼-in. flathead wood screws to attach the parts.

❾ Attach the cleats to the inside faces of the front and back rails with three #8 × 1¼-in. flathead wood screws per cleat **(See Photo F)**. Position the cleats so the rabbets face out from the base assembly, and the ⅛-in. rabbet shoulders are flush with the tops of the rails.

BUILD THE FACE FRAME, SIDE FRAMES & DOOR

❿ Cut the face frame stiles and rails to size.

⓫ Rout three ⅛-in.-deep flutes in each of the face frame stiles using a ¼-in. core box bit in a plunge router **(See Photo G)**. We cut the flutes by first building a jig from ¾-in.-thick plywood to hold a stile in place. On top of this plywood layer, we attached a second plywood frame to the first to serve as an edge guide for the router base when cutting the two outside flutes. By screwing a ½-in.-wide strip to one long inside edge of the frame, the jig then shifts the router into position to cut the center flute. We added short blocking to the ends of the jig frame to serve as references for starting and stoping the flute cuts (See *Face Frame Stiles Fluting*, page 53, for spacing the flutes). Experiment with this jig on scrapwood before you cut the actual workpieces.

⓬ Smooth the ends of the stile flutes and sand out any burns. *TIP: To sand out burns in the flutes, cut a pencil about 3 in. long and round over the eraser with sandpaper. Wrap a small piece of 180-grit adhesive-backed sand paper over the eraser and mount the pencil shaft in a drill. Operate the drill at low speed while you work the sandpaper tip into the flute ends* **(See Photo H)**.

13 Lay out three 3-in.-long hinge mortises in one edge of one face frame stile. Cut the hinge mortises. We used a router and straight bit and a jig built from scrap plywood. The jig straddles the edge of the stile and captures the base of the router to guide it in cutting each mortise. Clamp a stile on-edge in a bench vise, clamp the jig on the stile, over the mortise layout lines, and cut the mortises **(See Photo I).** You could also cut these mortises with a sharp chisel.

14 Lay out and drill holes for dowel joints in the ends of the face-frame rails. Drill two holes per joint. The ⅜-in.-dia. dowel holes should be ¾ in. deep and centered on the thickness of the rails. Space the holes on the rail ends, ½ in. from both edges.

15 Lay out and drill ¾-in.-deep dowel holes in the face frame stiles that will align with the holes you drilled in the rails.

16 Cut the rails and stiles for the side frames and door to size. Drill dowel-joint holes in the side frame rails and the door rails as you did for the face frame, but use the following spacing for the holes: side frame lower rails—½ in. and 1½ in. from the bottom edge; side frame upper rails—1 in. from both edges; door frame lower rail—¾ in. from both edges; door frame upper rail—¾ in. and 1½ in. from the bottom edge. Drill dowel holes in the side frame stiles and door stiles that align with pairs of holes in the corresponding rails.

17 Assemble the face frame, side frames and door. Apply glue and insert 1½-in.-long dowels in the face frame, side frame and door dowel joints. Also spread glue

Base

Spacer block

Top frame

Core box bit

PHOTO G: Rout three flutes into the face frame stiles using a ⅜-in. core box bit (See inset photo) in a plunge router. Guide the router against a shop-made jig, which consists of two parts: a base that holds a stile captive and a top frame that serves as an edge guide for the router and establishes the proper position of the two outside flutes. A spacer block attached to the top frame offsets the router to cut the center flute.

PHOTO H: Use a homemade flute sander to remove any burn marks and smooth the ends of the flutes. Wrap adhesive-backed sandpaper around the eraser of a pencil section chucked in your drill, and run the drill at low speed.

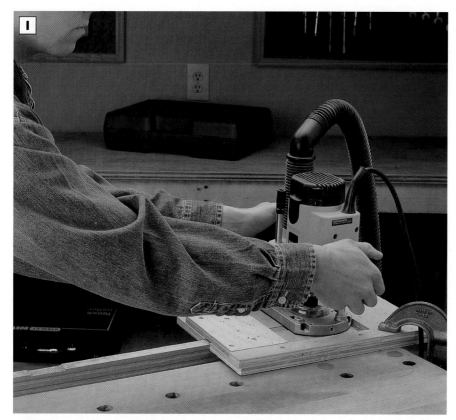

PHOTO I: To rout the hinge mortises, clamp a face frame stile on-edge in your bench vise. Clamp a shop-made hinge-mortising jig to the bench so it straddles the stile edge. Run the router around the inside of the jig frame to cut the hinge mortise.

PHOTO J: Glue the dowel joints and clamp together the rails and stiles for the face frame, side frames and door.

along the rail ends, then clamp up the assembly **(See Photo J).** Check the frames for square by measuring the diagonals; the frames are square when the diagonal measurements are equal.

PREPARE SIDE FRAMES & DOOR FOR CARCASE ASSEMBLY

18 Cut ⅜-in.-wide by ¼-in.-deep rabbets in the back edges of the side panels to accept the back panel as shown in the *Rear Corner Section View* drawing on page 53. We used a dado-blade set in the table saw to cut the rabbets. Attach a scrap plywood auxiliary fence attached to the saw's fence to keep the dado blade from cutting the metal saw fence.

19 Rout ¼-in.-deep, ¾-in.-wide dadoes for the bottom panel into the side frames. Space the dadoes 2 in. up from the bottoms of the frames. The dadoes can be cut on the table saw with a dado-blade set or with a straight bit in a router. If you use a router, guide the router with a straightedge.

20 Cut ⅜-in.-wide by ½-in.-deep rabbets in the side frames and door for the glass. We used a ⅜-in. piloted rabbet bit to cut around the inside edges of the side frames and the door frame. Cut the rabbets in several passes of increasing depth, to keep from burning the wood or damaging the router bit **(See Photo K).** Square the corners of the rabbets with a sharp chisel.

21 Lay out and drill holes for the adjustable shelf pins along the inside faces of the side frame stiles. Use a piece of perforated hardboard as a drilling guide, clamping it in the same position on both side frames when you drill so the shelf pin holes on the side frames will align with one another when the cabinet carcase is assembled. Circle the desired hole spacing on the hardboard to keep your drilling pattern uniform, and use a right-angle drilling guide to keep the shelf pin holes perpendicular to the side frames (**See Photo L**).

CUT THE GLASS RETAINER STRIPS

22 Cut stock to ⅜ × ⅜ in. to make the retainer strips that hold the glass panes in the frames. Crosscut the stops to length to fit into the rail and stile rabbets, then miter the ends of each strip at 45°, using a power miter saw or table saw and miter gauge. Label each stop on the back side and mark the same symbol on the corresponding rabbet surface as you fit each one, so it will be easy to sort the stops into their correct locations when you install the glass.

23 Drill ¹⁄₁₆-in.-dia. pilot holes in the glass retainer strips for nails. When you install the retainer strips, the brads used to attach them will slide easily into the pilot holes. You'll just need to tap or push the brads home into the door frame, which minimizes the risk of breaking the glass. *TIP: If you don't have a ¹⁄₁₆-in.-dia. drill bit, just nip off the head of one of the brads you plan to use to install the glass, chuck the brad in your drill, and drill your pilot holes.*

PREPARE THE BOTTOM PANEL & TOP SUPPORTS

24 Cut the bottom plywood panel to size. Resaw a piece of mahogany to ¼ in. thick to make the bottom front edge. Glue and clamp the bottom front edge piece to the front edge of the bottom panel to conceal the plywood

Piloted rabbet bit

PHOTO K: Use a ⅜-in. piloted rabbet bit (See inset photo) to cut rabbets on the insides of both side frames and the door frame. The rabbets create recesses for the glass panels. Make several passes of increasing depth with the router, until you reach the final depth (½ in). Then square the rabbet corners with a chisel.

PHOTO L: Drill shelf pin holes in the side frame stiles using a piece of perforated hardboard as a template and a drill guide to ensure perpendicular holes.

PHOTO M: Clamp up the cabinet frame temporarily and mark the biscuit locations on the top supports and side panels. Disassemble the cabinet and cut slots for #20 biscuits.

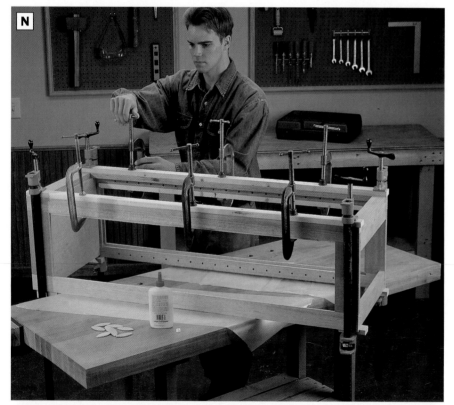

PHOTO N: Attach the face frame to the cabinet assembly with glue and biscuits, and clamp it up with a combination of C-clamps and pipe or bar clamps. Use full-length clamping cauls above and below the cabinet to distribute the clamping pressure evenly over the whole joint and to protect the cabinet parts from damage.

edges. Use full-length wood cauls to distribute clamping pressure evenly along the length of the edging. Allow the glue to dry.

25 Cut the top supports to size. The top supports align and reinforce the side frames and provide a surface to fasten the top panel in place. Cut a ¼-in.-wide, ⅜-in.-deep rabbet along the back edge of the rear top support. We used a dado-blade set in the table saw to make the cut. The rabbet provides a recess and fastening surface for the back panel and matches the rabbets you cut in the back edges of the side frames.

26 Temporarily clamp the carcase framework together, with the top supports in position between the side frames and the bottom panel in the side frame dadoes. Align the rabbet in the back edge of the rear top support with the rabbets in the side frames for the back panel. Mark locations for biscuit joints to attach the top supports to the side frames **(See Photo M),** then disassemble the carcase parts and cut #20 biscuit slots in the top supports and the side frames with a biscuit joiner. You can use dowel joints instead of biscuits if you prefer.

ASSEMBLE THE CARCASE

27 Finish-sand the side frames, top supports and the bottom panel. Glue and clamp the side frames, top supports and bottom panel together using biscuits or dowels in the top support joints. Allow the glue to dry and remove the clamps.

28 Cut the door stop and bottom back supports to size. Set the door stop into position beneath the front top support and mark the joint between the parts for two

#20 biscuits or dowels. Cut the slots or dowel holes, install the biscuits or dowels and glue the door stop to the carcase frame.

29 Position the bottom back support so it aligns with the back edge of the bottom panel. Attach the bottom back support to the carcase with glue and biscuits or dowels.

30 Lay out and cut #20 biscuit slots or dowel holes to attach the face frame to the front of the carcase. Clamp the face frame to the cabinet when you mark the joints to be sure the face frame remains aligned with the side frames and top supports.

31 Attach the face frame to the cabinet body. Spread glue into the biscuit slots and along the front edges of the carcase framework, then clamp the face frame to the carcase **(See Photo N).** Use long wood cauls between the clamp jaws and the face frame to distribute clamping pressure evenly.

32 Set the cabinet body on the base and drill countersunk pilot holes for screws to attach the parts. Drill three holes through the front base cleat and into the back of the bottom face frame rail. Drill three holes through the back base cleat and into the bottom back support. Temporarily attach the carcase to the base with six #8 × 1¼-in flathead wood screws.

HANG THE DOOR

33 Lay out and cut hinge mortises along the outside edge of the right door stile as you did on the face frame stile in Step 13. NOTE: *Be sure the door is oriented properly when you mark the hinge mortises; the wider door rail should be at the bottom of the cabinet.* Once the

PHOTO O: Cut hinge mortises into the edge of the face frame stile and attach the door to the cabinet with hinges and screws. Drill pilot holes for the screws to keep them from splitting the wood. Support the door from beneath as you attach the hinges.

Roman ogee bit

PHOTO P: Clamp the top panel to the workbench and use a Roman ogee bit to rout a profile around the side and front edges. Insert scrap plywood between the benchtop and the top panel to give clearance for the bit's pilot bearing.

Then finish-sand the rest of the cabinet top with 150-, then 180-grit sandpaper.

38 Position the top on the cabinet body. Adjust it so the back, flat edge of the top is flush with the back edge of the rear side frame stiles, overhanging the cabinet sides and front evenly. Clamp the top temporarily in position and drill countersunk pilot holes for #8 × 1¼-in. flathead wood screws up through the top supports and into the top. NOTE: *To allow the top panel to expand and contract, we made slotted screw holes in the top supports. To make slotted holes, drill pairs of holes side-by-side and connect them with a chisel.* Fasten the top to the cabinet with screws driven through the slotted holes. Check the fit, then remove the top for finishing.

39 Rip-cut and cross-cut the back plywood panel to size from ¼-in.-thick plywood. Set the mirror and back panel into place on the back of the cabinet body and check the fit of the parts. Then detach the cabinet from the base to prepare the parts for finishing.

PHOTO Q: Set the glass into the recess in the door, and nail the mitered retainer strips in place. We drilled pilot holes in the strips first to make driving the nails easier. A brad driver (shown here) allows you to push the nails into place rather than swing a hammer close to the glass.

mortises are cut, install the door on the carcase with hinges, drilling pilot holes for the hinge screws **(See Photo O).**

34 Check the fit of the door in the face frame opening and trim the door with a hand plane, if necessary, so there is an even ¹⁄₁₆-in. gap all around the door. Plane a slight chamfer around the front edge of the door frame, which will create a shadow line when the door is closed.

35 Lay out and drill holes in the edges of the door stile and face frame to mount the bullet catch and its latch opposite each other, but don't mount the hardware yet. Then remove the hinges from the door and cabinet body to prepare the wood parts for finishing.

ATTACH THE TOP & BACK
36 Edge-joint and glue up solid mahogany stock to make a panel for the cabinet top. The panel should be about about an inch oversize in length and width. When the glue dries, remove the excess glue with a cabinet scraper and cut the top to its final dimensions, as given in the *Cutting List,* page 52.

37 Install a piloted Roman ogee bit in your router. Clamp the top securely to your workbench and rout the ogee profile on the side and front edges of the top panel only, taking care not to let the ball-bearing pilot roll the bit around the back edge of the top **(See Photo P).** Sand the routed edges smooth by hand and remove any burn marks left by the router.

APPLY THE FINISH
40 Finish-sand all surfaces, and check carefully for any glue left on the wood, which will repel your stain finish.

41 Apply the wood stain of your choice to all inside and outside surfaces of the display cabinet parts, including the rabbets for the glass and mirror. We used mahogany stain. Topcoat the parts with three coats of polyurethane varnish, tung oil or Danish oil.

ASSEMBLE THE CABINET
42 Reattach the top to the cabinet carcase with screws driven up

through the top supports.

43 Install the glass in the door frame. Place the door frame on a padded worksurface with the rabbeted side facing up. Set the glass into the rabbets and insert the retainer strips around the glass. Attach the strips carefully using a small tack hammer or a brad pusher to drive the ¾-in. brads **(See Photo Q).**

44 Install the glass in the cabinet side frames. Position the cabinet so the side frame you are working on is facing down. Set the glass in place and attach the retainer strips with brads.

45 Install the mirror and back panel. Set the cabinet down on its front face with padding under it to protect the front edge of the top from damage. Clean the mirror and lay it into position on the back of the cabinet. Place the plywood back panel on top of it in the side-panel rabbets, and nail or screw the plywood into place, being careful not to damage the mirror.

46 Attach the base to the cabinet. Lay the cabinet on its back and place scrap 2 × 4 blocking under the cabinet to raise it off the worksurface. Slide the base into position and screw it to the bottom of the cabinet through the base cleats **(See Photo R).**

47 Mount the doorknob and bullet catch on the left door stile. Reinstall the hinges and hang the door on the face frame, making sure it opens and closes correctly. Install the door latch in the face frame and adjust the action of the catch and latch. *TIP: You can make minor adjustments to the door's position in its frame by shimming*

PHOTO R: Attach the base to the cabinet with screws driven through the pilot holes. Set blocks beneath the cabinet to allow clearance for the base.

behind a hinge with a piece of thick or thin paper or a matchbook cover, or by paring a hinge mortise a bit deeper with a small paring chisel. Apply small adhesive-backed felt dots to the inside left corners of the door frame to cushion it when it closes.

48 Insert the shelf pins in their holes in the side frames. Determine the spacing you need between the shelves by measuring the objects you want to display on each shelf. Don't crowd the height; allow a little extra headroom above the objects to permit easy removal.

49 Clean the glass shelves and set them on the pins inside the cabinet (you'll need to tilt the shelves to the side to get them in). We used ¼-in.-thick tempered glass

for the shelves instead of wood to enhance the mirrored effects inside the cabinet. Glass this thick can be quite expensive, but it's plenty strong and a good choice for small sections of shelving. Be sure to give the glass shop exact cutting dimensions when you buy it, and have them bevel and polish the razor-sharp edges.

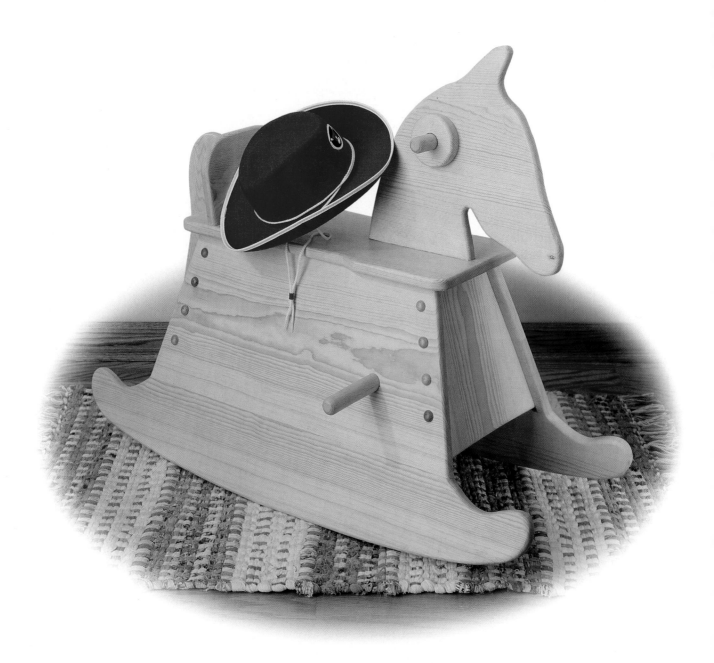

Rocking Horse

Build this trustworthy steed for a little cowpoke in your life, and you'll create a rocking toy that could well get passed down for generations to come. This rocking horse is made from standard-dimension pine available at any lumberyard or home center. With safety in mind, the design sports a wide base, shallow rocker curve, rounded edges and concealed fasteners.

Vital Statistics: Rocking Horse

TYPE: Rocking Horse

OVERALL SIZE: 20W by 36L by 28H

MATERIAL: Pine

JOINERY: Biscuits, dadoes, butt joints

CONSTRUCTION DETAILS:

· Rocking horse's wide, angled stance and gradual rocker profile make it less likely to tip
· Wide pine parts are edge-glued from narrower stock
· All edges are eased with ¼-in. roundover profiles or sandpaper
· Screw heads are capped with wood buttons or concealed underneath the rocker for safety

FINISHING OPTIONS: Clear water-based polyurethane varnish; could also be finished with child-safe paint

---

Building time

PREPARING STOCK
1-2 hours

LAYOUT
2-3 hours

CUTTING PARTS
4-6 hours

ASSEMBLY
2-3 hours

FINISHING
1-2 hours

TOTAL: 10-16 hours

Tools you'll use

· Jointer
· Table saw
· Jig saw, band saw or scroll saw
· Biscuit joiner
· Drill/driver and 1-in.-dia. spade bit
· Right-angle drilling guide
· Belt sander
· Router and ¾-in. straight bit, ¼-in. roundover bit
· Straightedge, bevel gauge or adjustable protractor gauge
· Bar or pipe clamps
· Compass
· Hammer and nailset

HANDYMAN Shopping list

☐ (1) 1 × 6 in. × 8 ft. pine
☐ (1) 1 × 10 in. × 8 ft. pine
☐ (1) 1 × 12 in. × 8 ft. pine
☐ 1-in.-dia. × 36-in. pine doweling
☐ 4d finish nails
☐ #8 flathead wood screws (1¼, 2-in.)
☐ ⅜-in.-dia. wood buttons
☐ #20 biscuits
☐ Wood glue
☐ Finishing materials

Rocking Horse

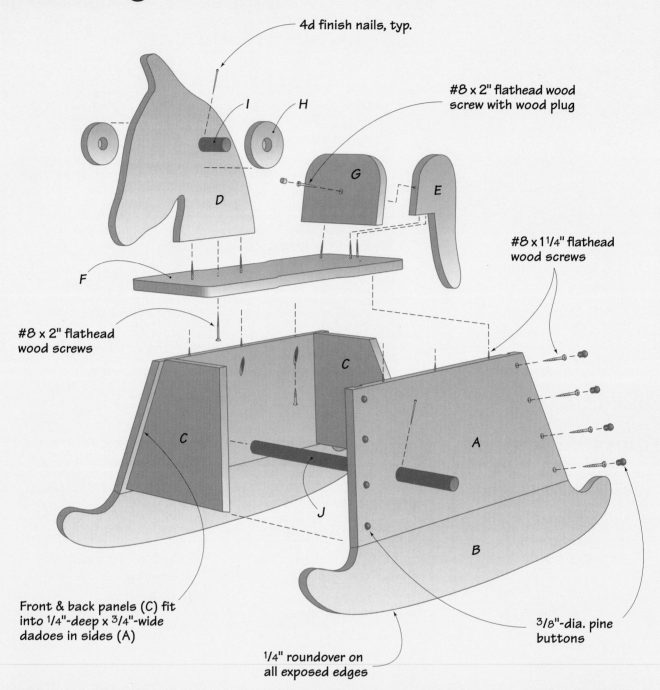

4d finish nails, typ.

#8 x 2" flathead wood screw with wood plug

I

H

G

E

D

#8 x 1¼" flathead wood screws

F

#8 x 2" flathead wood screws

C

C

A

J

B

Front & back panels (C) fit into ¼"-deep x ¾"-wide dadoes in sides (A)

¼" roundover on all exposed edges

3/8"-dia. pine buttons

Rocking Horse Cutting List

Part	No.	Size	Material	Part	No.	Size	Material
A. Sides	2	¾ × 10¼ × 24 in.	Pine	**F.** Seat	1	¾ × 9¼ × 22 in.	Pine
B. Rockers	2	¾ × 5 × 34¾ in.	"	**G.** Seat back	1	¾ × 5½ × 8⅜ in.	"
C. Front, back	2	¾ × 11¼ × 10 in.	"	**H.** Collars	2	¾ × 3¼ × 3¼ in.	"
D. Head	1	¾ × 13¼ × 14 in.	"	**I.** Handle	1	1-in. dia. × 6 in.	Pine dowel
E. Tail	1	¾ × 6 × 11½ in.	"	**J.** Footrest	1	1-in. dia. × 19½ in.	"

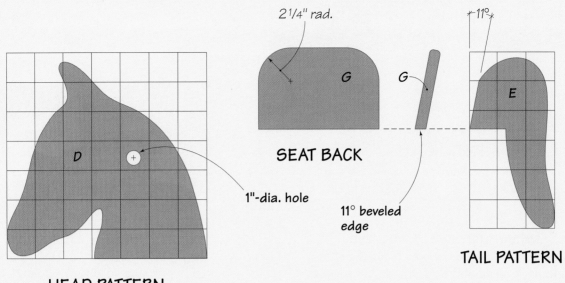

2¹⁄₄" rad.

SEAT BACK

G

1"-dia. hole

11° beveled edge

11°

E

TAIL PATTERN

D

HEAD PATTERN

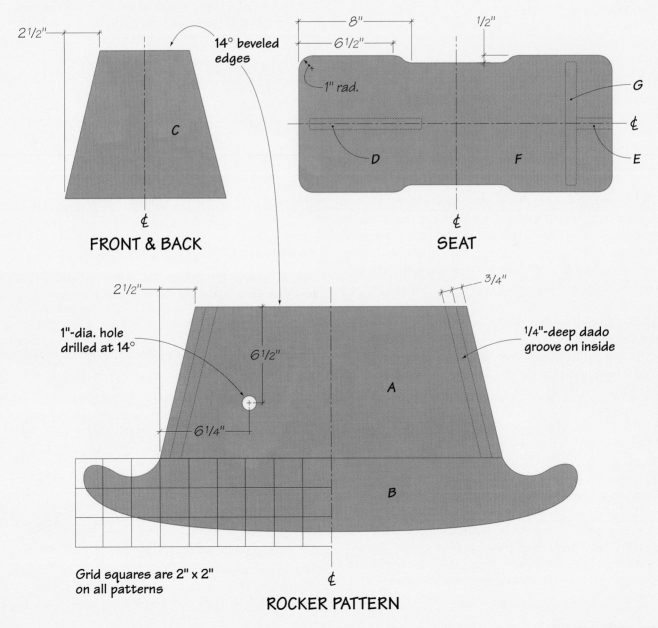

2¹⁄₂"

14° beveled edges

C

¢

FRONT & BACK

8"

6¹⁄₂"

1" rad.

1⁄₂"

G

D

¢

F

E

¢

SEAT

2¹⁄₂"

3⁄₄"

1"-dia. hole drilled at 14°

6¹⁄₂"

A

¹⁄₄"-deep dado groove on inside

6¹⁄₄"

B

Grid squares are 2" x 2" on all patterns

¢

ROCKER PATTERN

Make the sides & rockers

1 Edge-joint and edge-glue panels for the sides, front and back, head and tail. Rip- and cross-cut these panels to the final sizes given in the *Cutting List,* page 66.

2 On one of the two sides, make a reference mark for the footrest hole 6½ in. from one edge (we'll call this the top edge) and 6¼ in. from the closer end. The intersection of these lines marks the centerpoint for the hole. Mark the footrest hole on the other side, measuring from the opposite end you chose for the first side piece. The resulting footrest marks should mirror one another.

3 Lay out the angled ends of the sides by measuring 2½ in. from each end along the top edges of both side panels and drawing reference marks. Draw a straight line from each mark to the bottom corner of the closer end **(See Photo A).** Cut along the angled lines and smooth the sawn edges with sandpaper.

4 Cut dadoes on the inside faces (the face opposite the footrest marks) of the sides along the angled ends you cut in Step 3. Install a ¾-in. straight bit in a table-mounted router and set the bit depth to ¼ in. Set the fence ¾ in. from the bit. Use an angled pushblock to guide each side panel over the bit **(See Photo B).** You could also cut these dadoes on the table saw with a dado-blade set.

5 Joint one edge of the rocker stock and cut to size. Join the rockers to the sides. Lay the sides on your workbench so the dadoes face up. Set the jointed edge of a rocker against the bottom edge of each side so the rocker overhangs the side evenly on both ends. Mark four biscuit locations along the joint between the side panels and the rockers **(See Photo C).** Cut #20 biscuit slots at your reference marks, then

PHOTO A: Lay out the angled ends of the side pieces and draw lines from the top edges to the bottom corners. Note the opposite locations of the footrest "X"s on the two side pieces.

PHOTO B: Cut ¾-in.-wide, ¼-in.-deep dadoes on the inside faces of the side panels with a ¾-in. straight bit in the router. Use an angled pushblock to guide the workpiece and a featherboard to secure the workpiece against the router table.

PHOTO C: Mark center lines for biscuit slot locations to join the sides to the rockers. Make sure the sides are centered on the rockers. Assemble the parts with #20 biscuits and glue.

spread wood glue along the mating parts of the joint, insert biscuits into the biscuit slots, and glue and clamp the rockers to the sides.

6 Cut a 14° bevel along the top edge of each side assembly on the table saw, with the blade tilted to 14°. Cut the bevels with the dado side of the workpiece facing up. NOTE: *If you cut these bevels on the table saw, set your saw fence so the blade just clips the corner across the board's thickness; it should not shorten the overall height of the sides.*

7 Drill the footrest holes through the side panels at the footrest reference marks you made in Step 2. Chuck a 1-in.-dia. spade bit in a drill that is mounted in a right-angle drill guide and set the drill guide angle to 14° **(See Photo D).** Drill test holes first.

8 Lay out the rocker curves using the grid pattern on page 67 as a reference. Cut out the rocker shapes with a jig saw or a band saw.

9 Smooth the edges of the rockers with a belt sander. We clamped the two side panels together in our bench vise and gang-sanded them **(See Photo E).** Gang-sanding ensures that the rocker curves will match. Then round over all the side assembly edges, except the beveled top edge, using a router and a ¼-in.-radius roundover bit.

MAKE THE FRONT & BACK

10 Rip- and cross-cut the front and back glued-up panels to size. On one end of each panel (we'll call this the top end), make reference marks 2½ in. from either edge, and draw a line connecting these marks to the closer bottom corners (similar to the side layouts you did in Step 3).

11 Cut a 14° bevel along the top ends of the front and back, just as you did on the top edges of the sides in Step 6 **(See Photo F).**

12 Cut the angled sides of the front and back pieces using a jig saw or band saw. Round over the bottom edge of both workpieces with a router and ¼-in. roundover bit. The edges of the angled sides and top end should remain square. Finish-sand the rocking horse sides, front and back.

13 Attach the sides to the front and back with wood glue and four #8 × 1¼-in. flathead wood screws per joint **(See Photo G).** The front and back should fit

PHOTO D: Drill 1-in.-dia. holes for the footrest at a 14° angle through the sides, using a right-angle drill guide. Place a backer board beneath the workpiece to prevent tearout.

PHOTO E: Clamp the side assemblies together and gang-sand both rockers. Sanding the rockers side-by-side ensures that the rockers will match and gives the belt sander a wider surface on which to ride.

PHOTO F: Cut a bevel along the top edge of the front and back pieces with the table saw blade tilted at 14°. Use a featherboard clamped to the saw table and a pushstick to guide the workpieces.

PHOTO G: Attach the sides to the front and back with glue and four #8 × 1¼-in. screws per joint. Drill counterbored pilot holes for the screws to accept ⅜-in.-dia. buttons.

PHOTO H: Round over the edges of the seat, seat back, tail, head and collars with a ¼-in.-roundover bit in the router (See inset photo). Since the parts would be difficult to clamp, set the parts on a high-friction router mat to keep them stationary during routing.

Roundover bit

PHOTO I: Attach the head and tail to the seat, driving screws up through the bottom of the seat. Fasten the seat back to the tail. Use #8 × 2-in. flathead wood screws and glue.

into the side dadoes so the ends and edges of the four parts align at the top of the glued-up assembly where the seat will attach. Drill counterbored pilot holes for the screws, to accept ⅜-in.-dia. pine buttons.

ADD THE HEAD, TAIL & SEAT PARTS

14 Enlarge the head and tail patterns on page 67 to full size and transfer the patterns onto the stock for the head and tail. Mark the centerpoint for the handle on the head piece. Cut along the outlines for the head and tail with a jig saw, band saw or scroll saw, and sand the cut edges smooth. Drill a 1-in.-dia. hole for the handle through the head piece.

15 Cut the seat board to size from 1 × 10 pine and mark the seat board for the shaped recesses and rounded corners that are shown in the drawing on page 67. Cut the seat board to shape and sand the edges smooth.

16 Cut the seat back to size from 1 × 6 pine. Cut an 11° bevel along one edge of the seat back on the table saw. Lay out and cut the 2¼-in.-radius corners on the edge opposite the bevel edge. Smooth the cut edges with sandpaper.

17 Cut two 3¼-in.-square blanks for the handle collars. Connect the diagonal corners of each workpiece with straight lines, and mark the centerpoint where the lines intersect. Draw a 3¼-in.-dia. circle around these centerpoints with a compass. Drill a 1-in.-dia. hole through the centerpoint of each collar for the handle, and cut the circular collars to shape. Finish-sand the collars.

18 Round over the edges of the seatboard, collars, seat back, head and tail with a router and a ¼-in. roundover bit, except for the bottom edge of the head and seat back where each will attach to the seat, as well as the two straight edges of the tail **(See Photo H)**. Finish-sand all of these parts.

19 Attach the head and tail to the seat with glue and #8 × 2-in. flathead wood screws, driven through clearance holes in the underside of the seat **(See Photo I)**. Use the seat diagram on page 67 as a guide for positioning the head and tail. Position the head 1 in. back from the front end of the seat. Spread glue along the beveled edge of the seat back and set the seat back into place on the seat so it rests against, and is centered on, the tail. On the seat back, measure up 2¼ in. from the seat and drill a

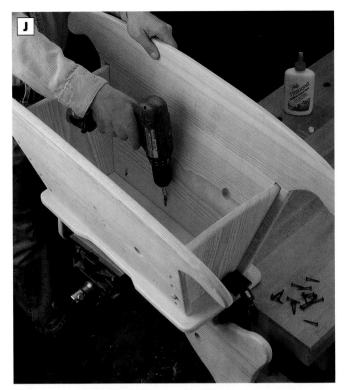

PHOTO J: Center the base on the bottom of the seat. Spread glue on the mating surfaces and drive #8 × 1¼-in. flathead wood screws up into the seat, through counterbored pocket holes, to attach the parts.

PHOTO K: Secure the footrest and the handle dowels with 4d finish nails driven at angles into the adjoining panels. Set the nails below the wood surface with a nailset. Glue the handle collars to the head.

counterbored pilot hole through the seat back into the tail. Attach the two parts with a 2-in. screw, cover the screwhead with a pine plug, and cut the plug off flush when the glue dries.

20 Attach the base to the seat with glue and six #8 × 1¼-in. flathead wood screws. Clamp the seat assembly upside-down in a bench vise and center the base on the bottom of the seat. Drill countersunk pocket holes through the base and into the seat to fasten the parts together **(See Photo J).**

FINISHING TOUCHES

21 Cut the dowels to length for the handle and footrest, and round over the ends with sandpaper. Finish-sand the dowels.

22 Install the footrest through the holes in the base and install the handle through the hole in the rocking horse head. Adjust both dowels so they protrude evenly on both sides. Lock the dowels in place with 4d finish nails driven at an angle. Set the nailheads below the surface of the dowels with a nailset **(See Photo K).** Slip the handle collars over the handle ends in the head and glue and clamp the collars to each side of the head.

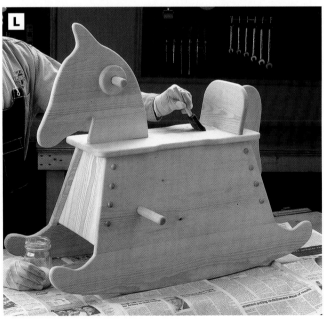

PHOTO L: Finish-sand any remaining rough edges and apply three coats of clear polyurethane varnish to all wood surfaces.

23 Glue pine buttons into the counterbored holes in the rocker base to conceal the screw heads.

24 Finish-sand any rough surfaces and apply three coats of water-based polyurethane or another child-safe finish **(See Photo L).**

Butcher-block Wine Bar

C ombine storage for wine bottles and wine glasses with a handy surface for serving your wine and *hors d'oeuvres* in one sleek project. The durable butcher-block top can be used as a cutting board for slicing cheese or fruit. The bar fits neatly against the wall and blends with just about any decorating scheme.

Vital Statistics: Butcher-block Wine Bar

TYPE: Wine rack with bar top

OVERALL SIZE: 30W by 15D by 35H

MATERIAL: Red alder

JOINERY: Edge-glued joints, butt joints reinforced with screws

CONSTRUCTION DETAILS:
- Butcher block-style top
- Three racks hold up to 15 wine bottles with a slight downward tilt
- Beveled stemware holders provide hanging storage for glasses
- Screw heads concealed with wood buttons

FINISHING OPTIONS: As shown, three coats of tung oil were applied to the entire project. If you plan to use the bar top as a cutting board, finish it separately with a non-toxic finish, such as salad bowl oil or special butcher block oil.

Building time

PREPARING STOCK
3-4 hours

LAYOUT
2-4 hours

CUTTING PARTS
2-3 hours

ASSEMBLY
1-2 hours

FINISHING
1-2 hours

TOTAL: 9-15 hours

Tools you'll use

- Planer
- Jointer
- Table saw
- Biscuit joiner
- Band saw
- Drill/driver
- Router with ¼-in. roundover bit
- Drill press
- 4-in. hole saw
- 1½-in. Forstner bit
- Bar or pipe clamps

Shopping list

- ☐ (2) 6/4 × 6 in. × 8 ft. red alder
- ☐ (2) ¾ × 6 in. × 8 ft. red alder
- ☐ #8 flathead wood screws (1½-, 2½-, 3½-in.)
- ☐ ⅜-in.-dia. wood buttons
- ☐ Wood glue
- ☐ Finishing materials

Butcher-block Wine Bar

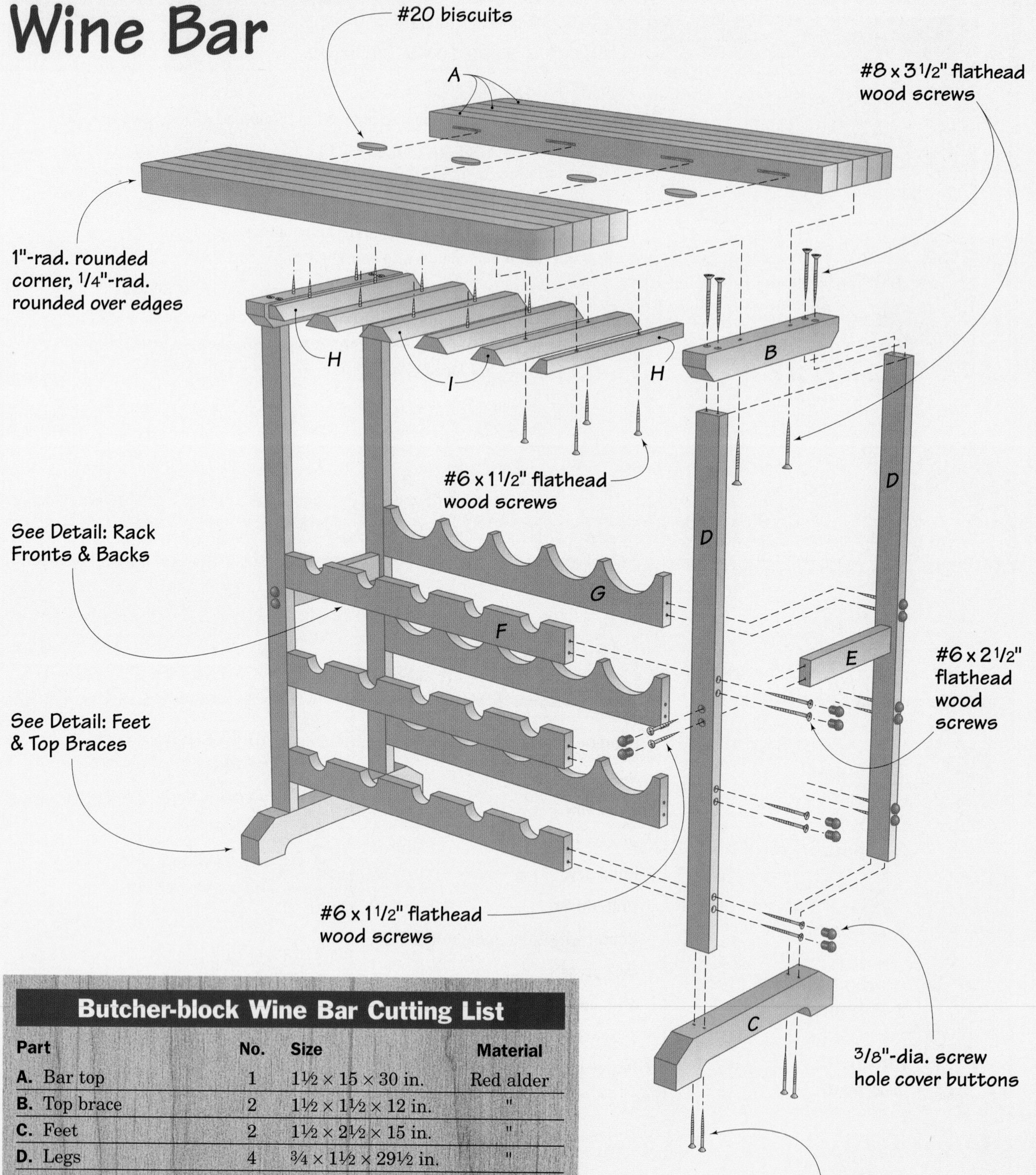

#20 biscuits

A

#8 x 3 1/2" flathead wood screws

1"-rad. rounded corner, 1/4"-rad. rounded over edges

H

I

H

B

D

D

#6 x 1 1/2" flathead wood screws

See Detail: Rack Fronts & Backs

G

F

E

#6 x 2 1/2" flathead wood screws

See Detail: Feet & Top Braces

#6 x 1 1/2" flathead wood screws

3/8"-dia. screw hole cover buttons

C

#8 x 3 1/2" flathead wood screws

Butcher-block Wine Bar Cutting List

Part	No.	Size	Material
A. Bar top	1	1½ × 15 × 30 in.	Red alder
B. Top brace	2	1½ × 1½ × 12 in.	"
C. Feet	2	1½ × 2½ × 15 in.	"
D. Legs	4	¾ × 1½ × 29½ in.	"
E. Spreaders	2	¾ × 1½ × 8 in.	"
F. Rack fronts	3	¾ × 2 × 22 in.	"
G. Rack backs	3	¾ × 3 × 22 in.	"
H. Stemware holder ends	2	¾ × 1¼ × 12 in.	"
I. Stemware holders	4	¾ × 2½ × 12 in.	"

 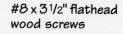

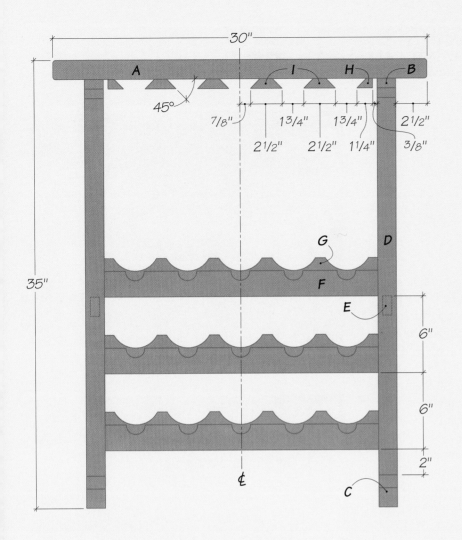

FRONT VIEW

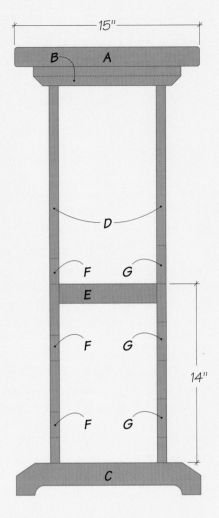

SIDE VIEW

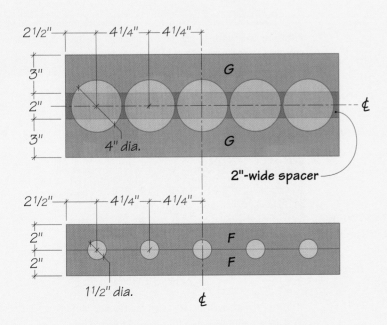

DETAIL: RACK FRONTS & BACKS

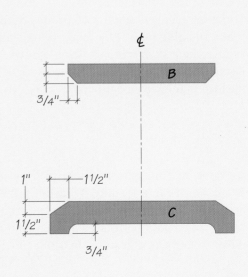

DETAIL: FEET & TOP BRACES

MAKE THE BAR TOP

The 1½-in.-thick bar top is built using butcher-block construction techniques. While a standard butcher-block surface (normally maple) is made with chunks of wood glued together with their edge-grain facing up, the bar top shown here consists of long wood strips (we used red alder) glued together with their face-grain edges up. In this way, it resembles a workbench—actually, the whole construction of this project is very much like a workbench.

1 We used unplaned, 6/4 red alder to make the butcher block top (so in reality, the top was slightly thinner than 1½ in. after we jointed and planed the boards). If you would like a full 1½-in.-thick top, you'll need to buy 6/4 stock and plane it to 1⅝ in. thick. Joint and plane the stock for the top so all sides are flat and square. Cross-cut it into ten 31-in.-long strips, and rip the strips to 1½ in. wide.

2 Spread glue evenly on the mating faces (not the edges) of the strips and glue the sections together. We assembled the top in two groups of five strips to make the glue-up a little more manageable and reduce the risk of warpage **(See Photo A).** Creating two narrower sections also allowed us to use a 12-in. surface planer to smooth out the top. NOTE: *Cutting biscuit joints between the strips will help keep them aligned during glue-up, but it isn't necessary from a structural standpoint.*

3 Wipe off glue squeeze-out with a wet rag (or, some people prefer to wait until it hardens, then scrape it off). Feed the two sections of blocks through the planer to smooth both faces of each, and plane them down to uniform thickness. OPTION: *Cut biscuit slots into each bar-top section to aid in alignment. Then, glue and clamp the two halves together.*

PHOTO A: Edge-glue the bar top sections together in two five-strip sections. You can use biscuit joints to help in the alignment if you want. Alternate clamps top and bottom to assure even clamping pressure.

PHOTO B: After edge-gluing the two sections together, use a sharp cabinet scraper to smooth out the seams between strips.

Roundover bit

PHOTO C: Round over the edges on the top and bottom of the bar top. We used a router with a ¼-in. piloted roundover bit (See inset photo). A high-friction router pad holds the top steady.

4 When the glue is dry, remove the clamps and level off the joints with a sharp cabinet scraper (**See Photo B).** Don't just focus on one area though, or it will become dished out. Scrape the entire surface of the bar top. Scraping with a cabinet scraper can remove material more quickly and neatly than sandpaper, and you'll end up with a smoother surface.

5 Cross-cut the bar top to 30 in. Check the width, and trim to 15 in. if it's too large. Use a compass or a circle template to draw 1-in.-radius roundovers at the corners. Cut the roundovers with a band saw or a jig saw, and sand smooth. Ease all edges with a router and a ¼-in. roundover bit (**See Photo C).** We held the bar in place during routing on a high-friction router pad, to keep from having to clamp it to the workbench.

MAKE THE BASE

6 Cut the workpieces for the top braces and feet to size (as shown in the *Cutting List,* page 74). Lay out the angled corner cuts on each part, using the *Feet & Top Braces* drawings on page 75 as guides. Also lay out the curved cutouts on the feet. Cut the parts to shape on a band saw (**See Photo D).**

7 The wine racks that are connected between the legs are made from opposing wood strips with cutouts for the wine bottle base on one side and the neck on the other side. As shown, we installed three sets of rack pairs that hold five standard wine bottles each. If you're looking for a little more storage capacity, you can eliminate the stemware holders on the underside of the bar top, and add another rack pair 6 in. above the upper rack shown in the plan. To make the semicircular cutouts for the neck, we found it was easiest to cut circular shapes into wider boards, then rip them in half. Start by cutting two boards to 4 × 22 in. for the fronts. Draw a centerline down the length of each board, then use the detail drawings on page 75 as guides for laying out centerpoints for the holes. Cut 1½-in.-dia. holes at the centerpoints in the front board, using a Forstner bit, a spade bit or a 1½-in.-dia. hole saw in the drill press.

8 Cut three boards to 3 × 22 in. for the back members of the racks. Cut a 2-in.-wide spacer from ¾-in.-thick scrapwood and clamp it between two of the boards. Mark a centerline on the scrap board, then lay out centerpoints for 4-in.-dia. holes along the centerline, according to the drawing on page 75. Cut the holes with a 4-in. hole saw (**See Photo E).** Cut

PHOTO D: Cut out the profiles for the feet and top braces on a band saw or with a jig saw. Use relief cuts and starter holes to make tight curves and keep waste out of the way of the saw blade.

PHOTO E: Drill 4-in.-dia. holes at the centerpoints on a 2-in.-wide spacer to make the semicircular cutouts for the bottle bases on the rack backs.

Blade guard removed for clarity

PHOTO F: Rip-cut the rack fronts in half to yield the finished parts with arched cutouts. The extra rack piece can be installed above the upper rack, along with a rack back, if you choose to eliminate the stemware hangers.

PHOTO G: Lay out reference lines on the edges of the legs to mark where the rack fronts and backs should be attached. For speed and accuracy, gang the legs together and mark them all at the same time.

PHOTO H: After attaching the rack members, attach the feet and the top braces so the legs are 8 in. apart on the ends of the base.

PHOTO I: Glue and screw the spreaders between the front and back legs. The tops of the spreaders should be level with the lower edges of the upper racks. All visible screw holes on the legs should be counterbored to accept wood buttons.

another spacer, clamp it to the third back rack board, and lay out and cut holes.

❾ Rip boards for the front rack in half along the centerline to create the racks with the bottleneck cutouts **(See Photo F).**

❿ Cut the four legs to size. Lay out the locations of the front and back racks on the inside edges of the legs, following the spacing shown on the *Front View,* page 75. You can mark all four legs at once by clamping them together, with the ends flush **(See Photo G).**

⓫ Finish-sand the racks, the feet, top braces and legs with 180-grit sandpaper.

⓬ Attach the racks to the legs with glue and two #8 × 2½-in. flathead wood screws. Drill counterbored screw holes for ⅜-in.-dia. wood buttons.

⓭ Attach the feet to the bottoms of the leg pairs with glue and #8 × 3½-in. flathead wood screws, driven through countersunk pilot holes in the undersides of the feet **(See Photo H).** The feet should be arranged so the insides of the legs are 8 in. apart. Attach the top braces to the legs the same way you attached the feet.

⓮ To keep the base from bowing (especially when loaded with wine bottles), we attached a spreader at each end of the assembly. The spreaders should be centered on the width of the legs, and the top edges should be level with the lower edges of the upper racks. Cut the spreaders to size, sand them, and attach them with glue and #8 × 1½-in. wood screws driven through counterbored pilot holes **(See Photo I).**

PHOTO J: Bevel-rip six strips of ¾-in.-thick stock at 45° and cross-cut the strips in 12-in. lengths to make the stemware holders and holder ends. The holders should be beveled on both edges, and 2½ in. wide on the wider face. The stemware holder ends should be beveled on one edge and be 1¼ in. wide.

INSTALL STEMWARE HOLDERS

15 We attached beveled wood strips on the underside of the bar top to function as stemware holders. To make the stemware holders, bevel-rip strips of ¾-in.-thick stock so they're 2½ in. wide, with 45° bevels on each edge **(See Photo J).** Cross-cut six pieces to 12 in. long. Rip two of the pieces to 1¼ in. wide to make the two end pieces.

16 Attach the stemware hangers to the underside of the bar top according to the spacing shown on *Front View,* page 75. The ends of each piece should be 1½ in. from the edges of the the bar top. Attach the stemware holders with #8 × 1½-in. wood screws driven through countersunk pilot holes in the holders, and into the underside of the bar top.

17 Center the bar top on the top braces and attach it with #8 × 3½-in. wood screws driven through the top braces and into the bar top **(See Photo K).** Do not use glue to attach the bar top.

FINISHING TOUCHES

18 Inspect the project and sand any surfaces that still need it. Ease all sharp edges with sandpaper. Apply a dab of wood glue to the wood plugs and tap them into the countersunk holes in the legs **(See Photo L).**

19 Apply the finish. We used three coats of tung oil. NOTE: *If you plan to use the bar top as a cutting board, finish it separately using linseed oil, salad bowl oil or butcher-block oil.*

PHOTO K: After the stemware holders are attached to the underside, screw the bar top to the top braces. Don't use glue to attach the top.

PHOTO L: Glue ⅜-in.-dia. wood buttons into the screw counterbores on the legs. The mushroom-cap-style wood buttons are used for decorative effect. If you prefer, you can use standard wood plugs and trim them flush with the surrounding wood.

Backyard Bird Feeder

Create a rest stop for feathered backyard visitors with this chalet-style bird feeder. Made of weather-resistant aromatic Tennessee cedar, our feeder features a removable roof for easy refilling of the seed hopper and contoured gables that give the design an Alpine flair. A generously proportioned seed tray provides plenty of room for several birds to dine together at once.

Vital Statistics: Backyard Bird Feeder

TYPE: Bird feeder

OVERALL SIZE: 12½W by 12½D by 13H

MATERIAL: Tennessee cedar

JOINERY: Butt and miter joints, some reinforced with screws or nails

CONSTRUCTION DETAILS:

· Feeder roof can be detached for easy filling
· Gravity-fed seed hopper means seed is dispensed automatically
· Designed to be hung, but could be mounted on a post instead

FINISHING OPTIONS: No finish is required, but clear UV protectant will minimize graying

Building time

PREPARING STOCK
2 hours

LAYOUT
2-4 hours

CUTTING PARTS
2-4 hours

ASSEMBLY
2-3 hours

FINISHING
1 hour

TOTAL: 9-14 hours

Tools you'll use

· Table saw
· Jig saw
· Scroll saw
· Power miter saw
· Drill/driver
· Bevel gauge
· Protractor
· Combination square
· Bar or pipe clamps
· C-clamps
· Spring clamps
· Hammer or pneumatic nail gun

Shopping list

☐ (1) ¾ × 6 in. × 6 ft. cedar
☐ (1) ¾ × 8 in. × 6 ft. cedar
☐ ½-in.-dia. hardwood doweling
☐ 4d galvanized finish nails
☐ 2-in. galvanized deck screws
☐ (1) ¼ x 2 in. galvanized eye-bolt, washer & nut (if feeder will be hung, but not if it is post-mounted)
☐ Moisture-resistant wood glue

Backyard Bird Feeder

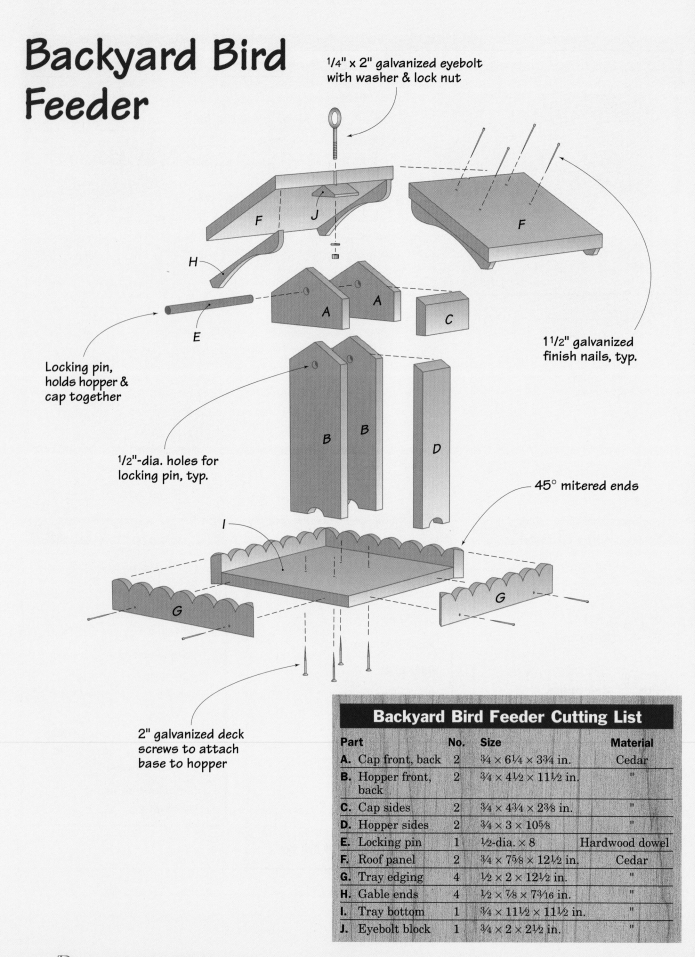

1/4" x 2" galvanized eyebolt with washer & lock nut

F

J

H

F

E

Locking pin, holds hopper & cap together

A

A

C

1 1/2" galvanized finish nails, typ.

B

B

D

1/2"-dia. holes for locking pin, typ.

45° mitered ends

I

G

G

2" galvanized deck screws to attach base to hopper

Backyard Bird Feeder Cutting List

Part	No.	Size	Material
A. Cap front, back	2	¾ × 6¼ × 3¾ in.	Cedar
B. Hopper front, back	2	¾ × 4½ × 11½ in.	"
C. Cap sides	2	¾ × 4¾ × 2⅜ in.	"
D. Hopper sides	2	¾ × 3 × 10⅝ in.	"
E. Locking pin	1	½-dia. × 8	Hardwood dowel
F. Roof panel	2	¾ × 7⅝ × 12½ in.	Cedar
G. Tray edging	4	½ × 2 × 12½ in.	"
H. Gable ends	4	½ × ⅞ × 7³⁄₁₆ in.	"
I. Tray bottom	1	¾ × 11½ × 11½ in.	"
J. Eyebolt block	1	¾ × 2 × 2½ in.	"

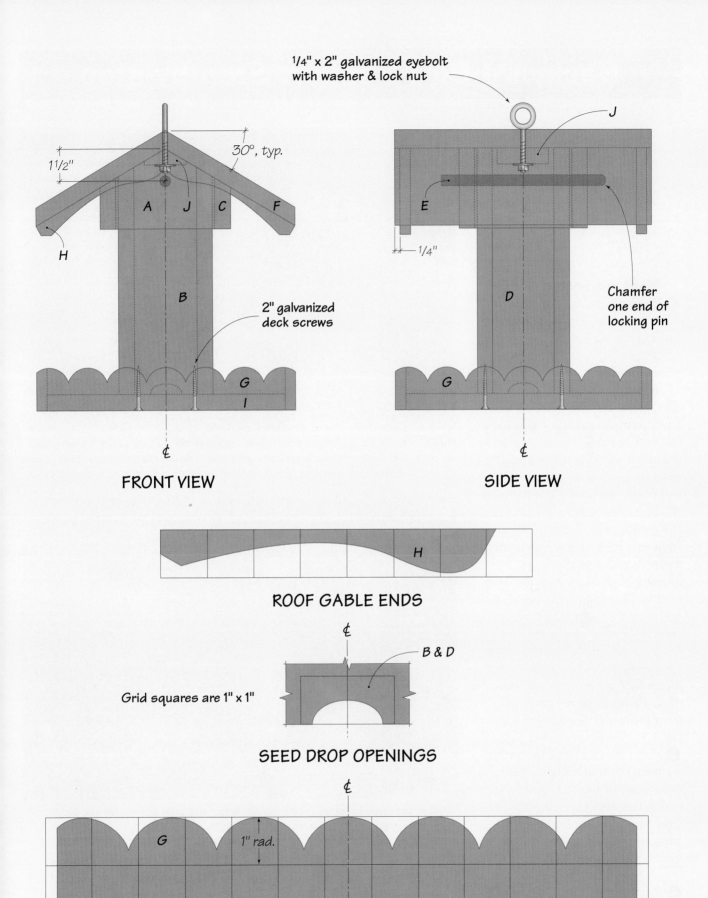

¼" x 2" galvanized eyebolt
with washer & lock nut

J

30°, typ.

1½"

A   J   C   F

H

E

¼"

B

Chamfer
one end of
locking pin

2" galvanized
deck screws

D

G
I

G

¢

¢

FRONT VIEW

SIDE VIEW

H

ROOF GABLE ENDS

¢

B & D

Grid squares are 1" x 1"

SEED DROP OPENINGS

¢

G

1" rad.

SCALLOPED EDGING

MAKE THE HOPPER & CAP

1 Rip- and cross-cut the hopper front, back and side pieces to size. Lay out the roof peaks at the top of each workpiece using a bevel gauge and protractor.

2 Lay out the cap parts as follows: To make the front and back cap pieces, cut a workpiece that's about 6¼ in. wide and about 12 in. long. Lay out a peak at each end of the workpiece **(See Photo A).** Make the miter cuts to form the peaks, then cross-cut the cap front and back to size, measuring down from the peaks. NOTE: *Making bevel cuts and miter cuts in small workpieces is dangerous and usually doesn't yield accurate results. To solve this problem, we bevel-cut and miter-cut the angles for the cap parts into longer workpieces that are more easily handled. Then we cut the parts out from the longer workpieces.*

3 Make the cap sides by cutting a workpiece that's 4¾ in. wide and about 10 in. long. Bevel each end of the workpiece at 30°. While your saw is set up for the bevel cuts, also cut a bevel in the top of each hopper side **(See Photo B).**

4 Cross-cut the cap sides to size, measuring down from the top of the bevel at each end of the workpiece to mark the cuts.

PHOTO A: Lay out the roof peaks on the hopper and cap fronts and backs using a bevel gauge set to 30°. Set the bevel-gauge angle with a protractor. Note that the cap front and back pieces are both laid out on one workpiece to make cutting the angles in these parts easier and safer.

PHOTO B: Cut bevels in the tops of the cap and hopper side parts on the table saw. Use the miter gauge to guide the workpieces through the blade.

5 Lay out the semicircular cutouts on the bottom of each hopper piece (See *Seed Drop Openings,* page 83). Make the cutouts with a jig saw or scroll saw **(See Photo C).**

6 Arrange the four cap parts together and check to see that the bevels in the side pieces align with the angles on the top of the cap front and back. Glue the cap pieces together with moisture-resistant wood glue, and clamp up the cap using wood cauls between the clamp jaws to distribute clamping pressure evenly. Glue and clamp the hopper pieces together (**See Photo D**).

INSTALL THE LOCKING PIN

To allow the cap to be easily detached from the hopper so the bird feeder can be filled, we inserted a dowel pin through the cap and hopper to secure them together.

7 Mark the location for the locking pin hole on the outside face of the cap front and back. The holes should be centered across the width of the cap and 1½ in. down from the roof peak.

8 Fit the cap over the hopper so the roof angles of the cap are aligned with the roof angles of the hopper. Hold the cap and hopper in position with spring clamps. Drill a ½-in.-dia. hole through both the cap and hopper at the pin-hole locations, then turn the assembly over and bore a hole at the other location mark (**See Photo E**). NOTE: *Gang-drilling the holes through both parts together will ensure that the holes are aligned. Hold the drill perpendicular to the cap faces when drilling the two holes.*

9 Cut an 8-in. length of ½-in.-dia. hardwood dowel for the bird feeder locking pin, and chamfer one end of the dowel by rolling it at an angle across a piece of sandpaper on your bench top. Insert the pin into the holes in the hopper and cap to check the fit.

ASSEMBLE THE ROOF

10 Cut the roof panels to length and width and bevel the sides at 30°.

11 Glue and nail the roof panels to the roof cap with 4d galvanized finish nails. You could also use a pneumatic nailer and galvanized brads (**See Photo F**). Spread moisture-resistant wood glue along the angled cap edges and between the mating surfaces of the roof panels where they meet at the roof peak. Align the roof panels over the cap so that the roof overhangs the cap evenly and the roof joint is tight at the peak. Then fasten the roof panels to the cap.

MAKE THE TRAY & GABLE TRIM

12 Rip- and cross-cut enough 2-in.-wide, ¾-in.-thick stock to complete the four pieces of tray edging and the four roof gable ends. Resaw the stock to ½ in. thick on your table saw (**See Photo G**). Use a

PHOTO C: Cut out the semicircular seed drop openings on the bottoms of the hopper front, back and sides, following the grid drawing on page 83. Use a jig saw or scroll saw to make these cuts.

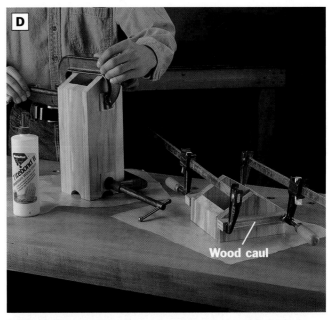

PHOTO D: Glue and clamp the parts together to assemble the bird feeder roof cap (right) and the hopper (left). Use moisture-resistant wood glue. Make sure the beveled side pieces align with the mitered angles on the fronts and backs.

pushstick to guide the workpieces and a featherboard to hold them tightly against the saw table and fence.

13 Rip the stock for the roof gable ends to ⅞ in. wide, and cross-cut the four gable-end blanks to 8 in. long. Cross-cut the four tray edging pieces to length, and bevel-miter the ends of the edging to 45°. Be sure the miter cuts do not shorten the overall length of the tray edging pieces.

PHOTO E: Align the roof angles of the cap with the roof profile on the hopper and clamp the parts together with spring clamps. Drill through the cap and hopper on both the front and back faces to create guide holes for the locking pin.

PHOTO F: Glue the roof panels to the cap, making sure the overhangs are equal. Then tack the roof in place with galvanized nails or brads. We used a pneumatic nailer for this task. Use a liberal amount of glue in the roof peak joint—the moisture-resistant glue will create a seal to keep the birdseed in the hopper dry.

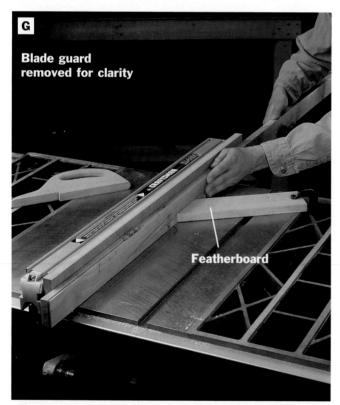

Blade guard removed for clarity

Featherboard

PHOTO G: Resaw the roof gable ends and the scalloped edging down to ½ in. thick on the table saw. Keep the stock tight against the rip fence and saw table with a featherboard, and use a pushstick to keep your hands away from the blade.

PHOTO H: Make templates for the curved gable trim and the scalloped edging. Trace the template onto the wood to create cutting lines, then cut with a scroll saw or a jig saw.

⓮ Make a hardboard template for the curved gable-end trim, and another for the scalloped tray edging, using the grid patterns on page 83 as a guide. Use the templates to trace the shapes of the roof gable ends and scalloped tray edging onto the workpieces. Cut the profiles with a scroll saw or jig saw (See **Photo H**).

⓯ Glue and clamp the gable ends to the underside of the roof panels so they meet at the roof peak. Apply glue to the flat edges of the gable ends and clamp them in place, set in ¼ in. from the roof ends. Use spring clamps to hold the gable ends in place.

⓰ Edge-joint and glue up ¾-in.-thick stock to make a 12 × 12-in. panel for the tray bottom. When the glue dries, rip- and cross-cut the panel to 11½ in. sq.

⓱ Glue and nail the scalloped edging pieces around the tray bottom with moisture-resistant wood glue **(See Photo I)**. Align the glued miter joints and see that the bottom edges of the tray edging are flush with the underside of the tray bottom.

⓲ Screw the tray to the hopper. Do this by clamping the hopper upside-side down in your bench vise. Center the tray on the hopper with the scalloped edging facing down. Mark locations on the tray bottom for the four screws that will attach the tray to the hopper. Drill countersunk pilot holes at these marks and fasten the tray to the hopper with 2-in. galvanized deck screws.

ATTACH HANGING HARDWARE

If you plan to hang your feeder like we did ours, proceed with the following steps. Otherwise, attach the tray of your feeder with #8 × 1½-in. galvanized screws, screwing down through the tray bottom and into the post. Set the post in the ground before you mount the bird feeder.

⓳ Cut a piece of blocking to fit inside the roof ridge and create a surface for attaching the eyebolt. The block should be about 2 in. wide and 2½ in. long, with the edges beveled to match the roof slope.

⓴ Spread waterproof wood glue over the beveled edges of the eyebolt block and position it underneath the roof ridge, centered on the roof cap. Allow the glue to dry, then drill a ⁵⁄₁₆-in.-dia. guide hole through the roof ridge and the eyebolt block. Install a ¼ × 2-in. galvanized eyebolt down from the roof top

PHOTO I: Glue the gable ends to the underside of the roof, and clamp them in place with spring clamps. Then glue and nail the scalloped edging pieces to the tray bottom.

Eyebolt block

PHOTO J: Glue the eyebolt block to the underside of the roof ridge. Drill a hole through the roof joint down through the block, then insert a galvanized eyebolt, washer and nut.

and through the eyebolt block. Secure the eyebolt to the roof with a washer and nut **(See Photo J)**.

㉑ No finishing materials are necessary, but if you want the project to retain its warm cedar tones, coat all exposed surface with a UV protectant wood sealer. Fill the hopper with birdseed, secure the roof with the locking dowel pin, and hang it by the eyebolt in a high-visibility location about 5 ft. from the ground.

Night Stand

Tuck remote controls and reading materials away neatly in this compact night stand project. Our simple design makes use of a variety of building materials including solid maple, maple and birch plywoods and melamine-covered particleboard. Most noticeable, however, is the curly maple veneer that spruces up the tabletop and drawer face to create decorative flair. Although it's designed to be used as a night stand, this project could suit a variety of other purposes, such as an end table or telephone table.

Vital Statistics: Night Stand

TYPE: Night stand

OVERALL SIZE: 18D by 20W by 26H

MATERIAL: Solid maple, maple (or birch) plywood, melamine plywood

JOINERY: Butt joints reinforced with biscuits, nails or screws; dado and miter joints

CONSTRUCTION DETAILS:
- Tabletop and drawer face are covered with maple veneer and edge-banding
- Curved sides, front edges and top
- Drawer outfitted with full-extension metal drawer slides that allow complete access to drawer contents
- Cabinet has a finished back so it can stand in the middle of a room

FINISHING OPTIONS: Three coats of polyurethane varnish, Danish oil or tung oil

Building time

PREPARING STOCK
2-3 hours

LAYOUT
2-3 hours

CUTTING PARTS
1-2 hours

ASSEMBLY
4-5 hours

FINISHING
1-2 hours

TOTAL: 10-15 hours

Tools you'll use

- Jointer
- Planer
- Jig saw or band saw
- Oscillating spindle sander or drum sander on the drill press
- Table saw
- Router with ¼-in. straight bit, ½-in. flush-trimming bit, ½-in. roundover bit
- Biscuit joiner
- Power miter saw
- Drill/driver
- Hand plane
- Bar or pipe clamps, C-clamps, wood screw clamps, spring clamps

Shopping list

- ☐ (1) ¾ in. × 2 ft. × 2 ft. melamine particleboard (melamine on one side)
- ☐ (1) ¾ in. × 2 ft. × 4 ft. maple plywood
- ☐ (1) ½ in. × 2 ft. × 2 ft. birch plywood
- ☐ (1) ¼ in. × 2 ft. × 2 ft. birch plywood
- ☐ (1) ¹⁄₃₂ in. × 2 ft. × 2 ft. maple veneer
- ☐ (3) 4/4 × 4 in. × 8 ft. maple
- ☐ #8 flathead wood screws (1-, 1¼-in.); 1 in. brads
- ☐ Wood glue
- ☐ #20 biscuits
- ☐ (2) 12 in. full-extension drawer slides
- ☐ (1) 1 × 1 in. wood knob
- ☐ Finishing materials

Night Stand

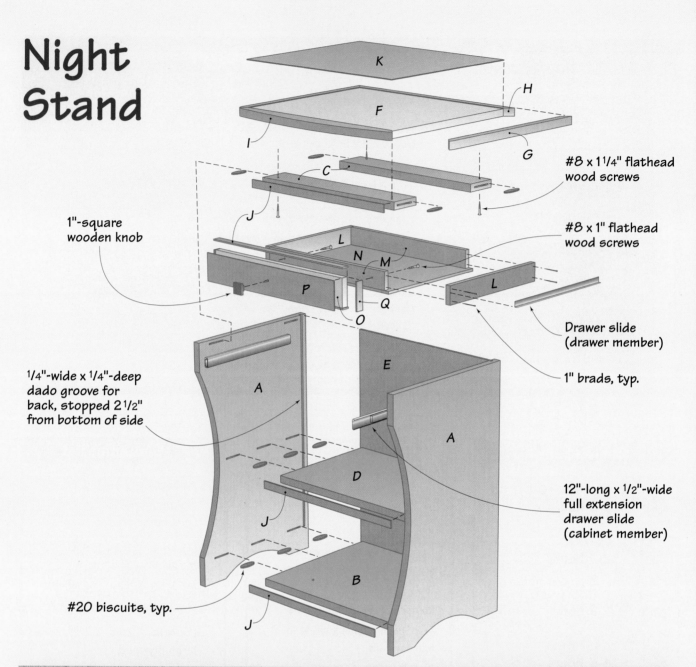

1"-square wooden knob

1/4"-wide x 1/4"-deep dado groove for back, stopped 2½" from bottom of side

#20 biscuits, typ.

#8 x 1¼" flathead wood screws

#8 x 1" flathead wood screws

Drawer slide (drawer member)

1" brads, typ.

12"-long x ½"-wide full extension drawer slide (cabinet member)

Night Stand Cutting List

Part	No.	Size	Material
A. Sides	2	¾ × 15½ × 25¼ in.	Maple
B. Bottom	1	¾ × 15⅛ × 17 in.	Maple plywood
C. Top supports	2	¾ × 3 × 17 in.	"
D. Shelf	1	¾ × 11⅞ × 17 in.	"
E. Back	1	¼ × 17½ × 22½ in.	"
F. Top core	1	¾ × 15⅝ × 18½ in.	Melamine
G. Top edging (sides)	2	13⁄16 × ¾ × 17⅛ in.	Maple
H. Top edging (back)	1	13⁄16 × ¾ × 20 in.	"
I. Top edging (front)	1	13⁄16 × 15⅝ × 20 in.	"
J. Edging	6	⅛ × ⅞ × 17¼ in.	"
K. Top veneer	1	1⁄32 × 8½ × 19½ in.	Maple
L. Drawer sides	2	½ × 1¾ × 12 in.	Birch plywood
M. Drawer front, back	2	½ × 1¾ × 15 in.	"
N. Drawer bottom	1	¼ × 12 × 16 in.	"
O. Drawer face core	1	¾ × 2¾ × 16⅝ in.	Melamine
P. Drawer face veneer	1	1⁄32 × 3 × 17 in.	Maple
Q. Drawer face edging (ends)	2	⅛ × 13⁄16 × 3 in.	Maple

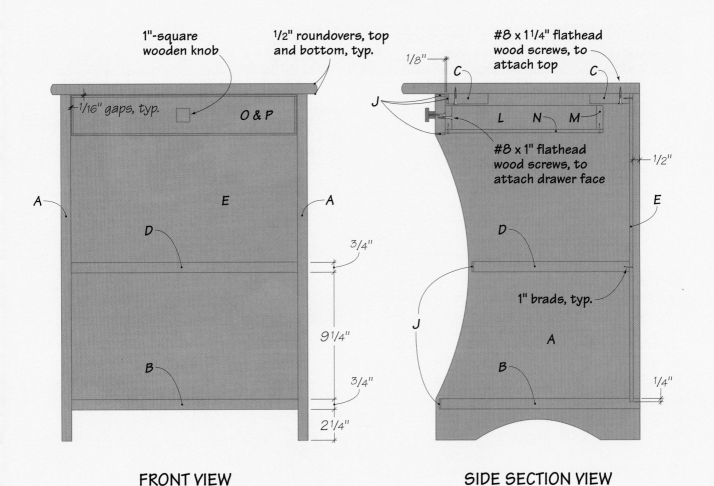

1"-square wooden knob

1/2" roundovers, top and bottom, typ.

#8 x 1¼" flathead wood screws, to attach top

1/16" gaps, typ.

O & P

1/8"

C   C

J

L   N   M

#8 x 1" flathead wood screws, to attach drawer face

A   A

1/2"

E   E

D   D

3/4"

1" brads, typ.

9¼"

A

B   B

3/4"

1/4"

2¼"

FRONT VIEW

SIDE SECTION VIEW

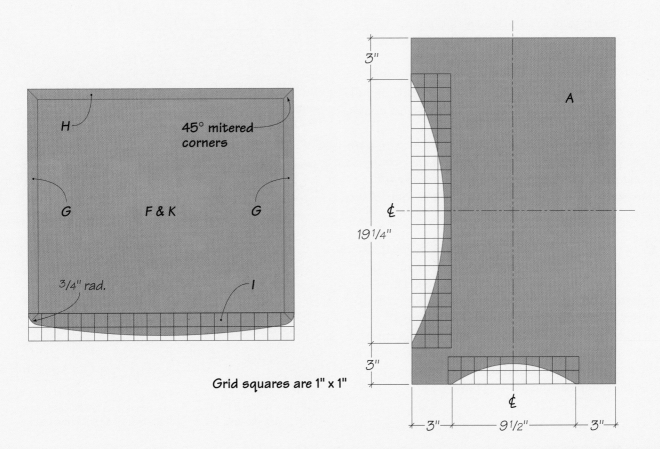

H

45° mitered corners

G   F & K   G

3/4" rad.

I

Grid squares are 1" x 1"

3"

A

¢

19¼"

3"

¢

3"   9½"   3"

MAKE THE SIDES

1 Edge-glue panels to make the sides. First, surface-plane the 4/4 maple stock you plan to use for the side panels to ¾ in. thick and joint the edges. Since the side panels are 15½ in. wide, we used four 4-in.-wide boards per side panel. Cross-cut the boards to 26 in. long. Glue up each side panel with bar or pipe clamps, alternating the clamps above and below the panels to distribute clamping pressure evenly. After the glue dries, scrape and sand the panels smooth, then cut them to final size.

2 Lay out the curved shapes on the front and bottom edges of one side, using the grid drawings on page 91 as guides. Make the cutouts with a jig saw or band saw, then use the side as a template to trace cutting lines onto the other side **(See Photo A).**

3 Clamp the two sides together and gang-sand them to the layout lines, using an oscillating spindle sander **(See Photo B).** *TIP: If you don't have access to a spindle sander, you can still make identical curves in the sides. Sand one side panel smooth with a drum sander or by hand-sanding. Then, clamp the two sides together and use a flush-trimming bit in your router to duplicate the curves of the sanded side onto the other unsanded side.*

4 Rout a ¼-in.-wide by ¼-in.-deep dado for the back panel along the inside face of each side panel. Locate the dado ½ in. in from the back edge of each side, and stop the groove 2½ in. from the bottom. Use a router with a ¼-in. straight bit, and clamp a straightedge to the side panel to guide the router as you make the cuts **(See Photo C).** Make a mark on the straightedge or clamp on a stopblock to ensure the dado stops at the 2½-in. point.

PHOTO A: Lay out curves on the sides, and cut them out with a jig saw or a band saw.

PHOTO B: To smooth the profiles on the sides (and to make them identical), we clamped the sides together and gang-sanded them on an oscillating spindle sander.

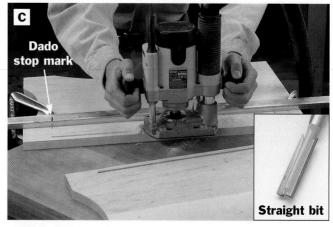

Dado stop mark

Straight bit

PHOTO C: Rout ¼ × ¼ in. dadoes along the inside faces of the sides, ½ in. in from the back edges, using a ¼-in. straight bit (See inset photo). Stop the cuts 2½ in. from the bottom edges of the sides.

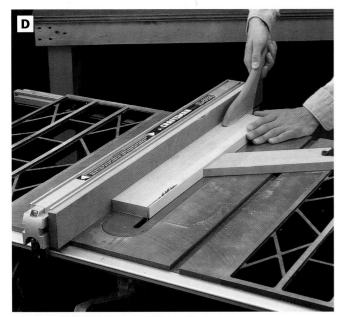

PHOTO D: Resaw ⅛-in.-thick edging strips from 4/4 maple stock, using a table saw or band saw. Joint the cut edge of the board flat before you rip each edging strip.

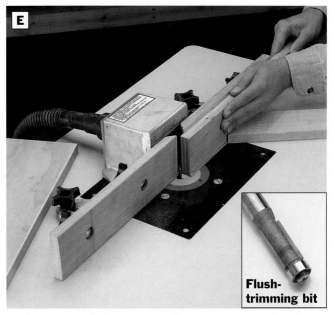

Flush-trimming bit

PHOTO E: Trim the ⅛-in.-thick edging flush with the plywood on the shelf, bottom and front top support using a piloted flush-trimming bit (See inset photo). Secure the workpieces with a featherboard.

ASSEMBLE THE CARCASE

5 Cut the bottom, top supports and shelf to size from maple plywood.

6 Resaw strips of ⅛-in.-thick edging from 4/4 maple stock that's at least 17¼ in. long. Before resawing, joint one edge of the maple stock, then plane the top and bottom faces until it's ⅞ in. thick. Resaw six strips of edging, jointing the cut edge of the board after you rip each strip of edging **(See Photo D).** This will give you enough edging for the front edge of the front top support, drawer face top and bottom, the front edge of the shelf, and the front and back edges of the bottom.

7 Glue edging strips to the front and back edges of the bottom, the front edge of the shelf and the front edge of a top support. Spread glue along the jointed face of the edging and the mating plywood edge. Use four bar or pipe clamps to clamp the edging on the panel, spacing the clamps evenly along the length of the glue joint. Insert long wood cauls between the jaws of the clamps and the edging to distribute clamping pressure evenly. As you tighten the clamps, you'll need to readjust the edging, if it shifts, to make sure it overhangs evenly all around. As a clamping option, you could also tape the edging into place with electrical tape as we do in the nesting table project, page 46.

8 Trim the top and bottom of the edging strips flush with the faces of the panels **(See Photo E).** Do the trimming on a router table using a ½-in.-dia. flush-trimming bit. Set the router table fence flush with the bearing on the bit to make the trim cuts, and clamp a featherboard to the table to keep the workpieces held tightly against the fence. Trim the edging flush with the ends of each workpiece using a fine-toothed back saw.

9 Rout a ¼ × ¼-in. dado across the top face of the bottom panel for the back. Position the dado ½ in. in from the back edge of the bottom panel, and cut the groove with a router and a ¼-in. straight bit.

10 Lay out and cut #20 biscuit joints in all the parts to join the top stretchers, shelf and bottom to the side panels. Use one biscuit in the end of each top support and three biscuits per end for the bottom and shelf joints. Center the biscuits on the thickness of the supports, shelf and bottom, and use a straight-edge to guide the biscuit joiner when cutting slots in the side panels **(See Photo F).** NOTE: *Locate the joints for the back top support so the back edge of the support is flush with the front edge of the back-panel dadoes in the side panels.*

11 Cut the back panel to size from ¼-in.-thick plywood. Finish-sand both faces, as well as the rest of the parts.

PHOTO F: Cut biscuit slots in the sides and in the ends of the bottom, top stretchers and shelf for assembling the carcase. Clamp a plywood straightedge to the side panels to help align the base of the biscuit joiner when cutting biscuit slots in the side panels.

PHOTO G: After gluing and clamping the carcase together, slide the back into the side panel and bottom grooves. Loosen the clamps a bit and adjust the carcase as necessary to square it up so the top edge of the back is flush with the top edge of the rear top stretcher. Then re-tighten the clamps and nail the back to the rear top support with three or four 1-in. brads. No glue should be used with the back panel.

⓬ Assemble the carcase. Spread glue along the edges of the top supports, shelf and bottom and into the biscuit slots. Spread glue into the biscuit slots in the side panels. Clamp the carcase parts together, making sure the parts are properly aligned (**See Photo G**).

⓭ Before the glue sets in the carcase assembly, slide the back panel (without glue) into the dadoes in the side panels and bottom. If the dadoes are exactly ¼ in. deep and the back panel is cut squarely, you should be able to slide the back in from the top and square the cabinet up by flushing the top edge of the back with the top edge of the rear top support. Make any adjustments necessary to square the carcase by adjusting the clamps. Attach the back to the top back stretcher with three or four evenly spaced 1-in. brads. Set the brads below the surface with a nailset and fill the holes with wood putty.

APPLY THE TABLETOP VENEER

When you apply veneer to any wood surface, the opposite surface must be veneered also, to keep the panel from warping. On the tabletop and drawer face in this project, we're using particleboard covered on one side with melamine. We'll apply the veneer to the unfinished side of the particleboard, so the melamine will be opposite the veneer.

⓮ Cut the tabletop to size from melamine stock.

⓯ Select the veneer sheets you'll use for the table-top. We used curly maple veneer for extra visual interest. Chances are you won't find a single 16-in.-wide sheet, so you'll need to join two narrower pieces of veneer together as we show here. If you have two consecutively cut sheets from a *flitch* (a pile of veneers stacked in the order they were sliced from the log), the grain on one piece will mirror the grain pattern on the other piece. Arrange the two pieces so that the grain matches along the joint between the veneer sheets (called *book-matching*). If you have one long sheet of veneer, cut two 20-in. sections with similar grain pattern and lay them side-by-side in different configurations to determine which arrangement looks most pleasing.

⓰ Cut the adjoining edges of the veneer sheets. Each veneer sheet needs to have a straight and square edge so the seam between the sheets will be as tight and unnoticeable as possible. Here are two methods for trimming the veneer joint:

Method 1: With the sheets lying side-by-side, flip one sheet over on top of the other, as if you're closing a book. Align the edges and clamp them between two sheets of plywood or particleboard, leaving the edges that will join together protruding slightly. Lay a jointing plane or jack plane on its side, with the sole of the plane against the edges of the plywood. Run the plane along the veneer edges, trimming them until they are jointed straight and even. *TIP: Be cautious on the first couple of passes. If the veneer grain starts tearing out, try planing from the other direction. If the edge is grossly uneven, unclamp the plywood and back off the veneer overhang so only a little protrudes. Then reclamp and plane the veneer edge in two stages to avoid cracking the loose, flapping sheets.*

Method 2: Clamp the veneer sheets between smooth-edged sheet goods (like medium-density fiberboard or high-quality hardwood plywood). Set a router with a flush-cutting bit on the stack and run the pilot bearing along the lower board's edge to joint the edges of the veneers.

17 Unclamp the setup and lay the veneers side-by-side with the jointed edges together and the grain and figure matched up to your satisfaction. On the top face of the veneer, place a short strip of low-adhesion masking tape across the joint at each end and another strip in the middle. If you stretch the tape slightly as you lay it down, it'll pull the joint tight. Then, run a long strip of tape down the length of the joint **(See Photo H).** A second option for securing the veneer together is to use veneer tape (See *Tip,* below).

18 Glue the maple veneer to the tabletop panel. Apply regular wood glue to the particleboard side of the tabletop core panel (Do not apply glue to the veneer, or it'll immediately curl up into a roll). We

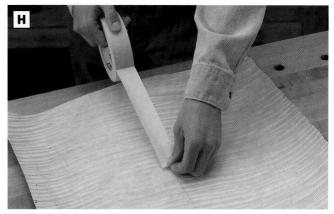

PHOTO H: Tape the jointed edges of the veneer together. Use short strips of tape to hold the joint tight. Then lay a strip down the entire length of the seam.

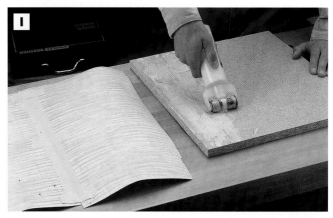

PHOTO I: Apply an even, light coat of glue to the unfinished particleboard face of the melamine board. Because the glue sets up quickly, have the veneer and your veneer press close at hand.

PHOTO J: Clamp the veneer to the glued-up panel in a homemade caul-and-particleboard plate veneer press. Allow a few minutes for the glue to squeeze out, then check to see if the clamps need tightening again. Let the glue dry for at least four hours before you remove the veneered panel from the press.

USING VENEER TAPE

Water-moistened veneer tape, available from most woodworking and veneer suppliers, is easier to remove than masking tape after it's been clamped under pressure—just wet it again and it peels right off with a cabinet scraper. Use a few strips of masking tape to hold the veneer together while you place strips of veneer tape across the seam. Then remove the masking tape and lay a strip of veneer tape along the length of the joint.

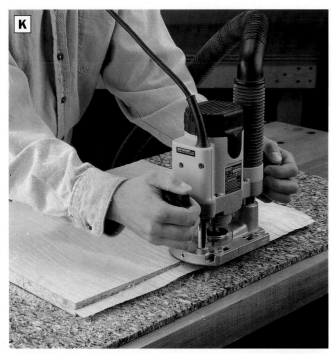

PHOTO K: Trim overhanging veneer with a router and a flush-trimming bit so the edges are flush with the tabletop.

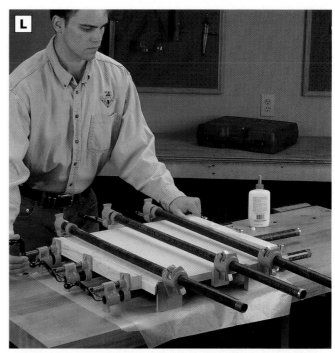

PHOTO L: Glue and clamp the edging to the tabletop, using #20 biscuits to keep the parts aligned. Match up the miters. NOTE: *The long miters on the wider front edging will protrude past the sides.*

used a glue bottle with dispenser rollers, but a foam paint roller or even a finely notched trowel would also work to spread the glue. Completely cover the panel surface with a thin, even coating of glue **(See Photo I).**

⑲ Position and clamp the veneer in place. Lay the veneer on top of the core panel with the tape facing up and immediately clamp the veneer to the core between two pieces of plywood or particleboard. The sheet goods will act as a veneer press, applying even pressure over the whole veneer surface. Use wood cauls across the setup to distribute clamping pressure **(See Photo J).** TIP: *Since glue dries quickly, it pays to have the press ready and everything close at at hand before you spread the glue. It's also a good idea to slip a sheet of waxed paper between the veneer and the top plate of the veneer press; glue squeeze-out will occur through the wood grain of the veneer, which can bond the veneer to the top plate.* Leave the veneered panel in the press for at least four hours if using yellow or white glue—overnight is best.

⑳ Trim the veneer flush with the edges of the tabletop core panel. First remove the veneered tabletop from the press and use a router with a flush-cutting bit to trim off the overhanging veneer on all the tabletop edges **(See Photo K).**

APPLY THE TABLETOP EDGING

㉑ Cut the tabletop edging to size from solid-maple stock. Cut 45° miters on the ends of the four edging pieces with a power miter saw or a table saw and miter gauge.

㉒ Lay out and cut biscuit joints for #20 biscuits, to help align the edging with the top surface of the tabletop. Apply glue to the edging and miters and into the biscuit slots. Clamp the edging to the tabletop with bar or pipe clamps **(See Photo L).** Clean up squeeze-out with a wet rag.

㉓ Transfer the grid drawing for the tabletop front edge profile (page 91) to the tabletop panel and use it as a guide for laying out the front edge profile. Cut along the curved layout line with a jig saw or band saw, and sand the sawn edges smooth. Then, use a router with a ½-in.-radius roundover bit to round over the top and bottom edges of all edging strips (See *Front* and *Side Section Views,* page 91). Finish-sand the curved edges and the top face just enough to level the surface and smooth the grain, being careful not to sand through the veneer.

MAKE & INSTALL THE DRAWER

㉔ Cut the drawer sides, front and back to size from ½-in. plywood. Assemble the drawer parts with glue and 1-in. brads so the drawer front and back butt

PHOTO M: Clamp the drawer face in position on the drawer front. Drill countersunk pilot holes and drive two 1-in. flathead wood screws to join the parts.

PHOTO N: Install the full-extension metal drawer slides and hang the drawer in the cabinet carcase. Be sure there is an even overhang between the drawer face and the cabinet carcase.

against the drawer sides at the corner joints. Cut the plywood drawer bottom to size. Sand all drawer surfaces smooth, then use glue and 1-in. brads to attach the drawer bottom to the drawer. Use the drawer bottom to square the drawer box before you fasten the bottom in place.

㉕ Cut the drawer face core an inch or so larger than the final dimensions given in the *Cutting List*, page 90, select a sheet of veneer for the drawer face and cut it oversize as well. Glue the drawer face veneer to the drawer face core on the particleboard side, using a smaller veneer press and the veneer gluing methods you used for the tabletop.

㉖ Cut the drawer face to finished size. Rip-cut and cross-cut ⅛-in.-thick edging pieces for the drawer face ends. Glue and clamp the end edging in place. When the glue dries, remove the clamps and trim the edging flush with the drawer face edges. Glue and clamp the top and bottom edging pieces you cut earlier to the drawer face, and trim the edging flush when the glue dries.

㉗ Finish-sand the drawer face. Tack it into place on the drawer box (**See Photo M**). Allow even overhangs at the ends of the drawer face. The top of the drawer face should sit ¹⁄₁₆ in. below the tops of the carcase side panels. The bottom edge of the drawer

face, minus the edging, should be flush with the bottom of the drawer box.

㉘ Hang the drawer at the top of the night stand opening, following the manufacturer's instructions for attaching the metal drawer slides (**See Photo N**). We used two 12-in. full-extension drawer slides.

FINISHING TOUCHES

㉙ Finish-sand any remaining rough spots and ease all sharp edges. Remove the drawer hardware.

㉚ Apply the finish of your choice to all parts. We used three coats of clear polyurethane varnish to enhance the natural color of the maple.

㉛ Reinstall the drawer slides and fasten the wooden drawer knob in place. Center the knob on the drawer face and attach it, screwing through the drawer front.

㉜ Attach the tabletop. Position the tabletop on the carcase so that the back is even with the carcase back panel and the sides and front overhang evenly. Attach the tabletop to the carcase with #8 × 1¼-in. flathead screws, screwing up through countersunk pilot holes in the top supports and into the tabletop.

Turned Table Lamp

Graceful, sophisticated lines and rich wood tones accentuate this charming table lamp, which could be a beautiful addition to the corner of a table or desk in your home. Our design is constructed of face-glued walnut and finished with oil to bring out the strong wood grain pattern. Although it's a hardwood, walnut turns beautifully on a lathe, making it a perfect project for beginning and seasoned wood turners alike.

Vital Statistics: Turned Table Lamp

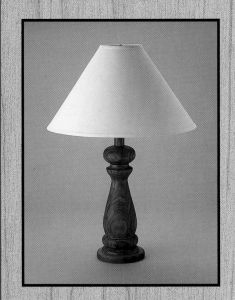

TYPE: Lamp

OVERALL SIZE: 6Dia. by 15H

MATERIAL: Walnut

JOINERY: Face-glued turning blank

CONSTRUCTION DETAILS:

· Face-glued, solid walnut lamp body
· Wiring hole is actually a pair of dadoes in the lamp base halves, cut before the base is laminated together
· Filler blocks glued into ends of wiring hole to mount lamp body blank on lathe chuck. Blocks are drilled out after lamp body is turned

FINISHING OPTIONS: Tung oil, Danish oil or three coats of polyurethane varnish

---

Building time

PREPARING STOCK
1-2 hours

LAYOUT
1-2 hours

CUTTING PARTS
2-3 hours

ASSEMBLY
1-2 hours

FINISHING
2 hours

TOTAL: 7-11 hours

Tools you'll use

· Jointer
· Table saw with dado-blade set
· Band saw
· Lathe
· Lathe tools: roughing gouge, parting tool, skew chisel, round-nose scraper
· Drill press
· Router with ⅜-in. roundover bit
· Scroll saw or coping saw
· Calipers
· ¼-, 1-in. Forstner bit
· Hack saw, metal file
· Bar or pipe clamps

Shopping list

☐ (1) 6/4 × 6 in. × 6 ft. walnut
☐ (1) ⅜-in.-dia. × 16-in.-long threaded rod
☐ (1) Lamp light socket
☐ (1) 8 in. lamp harp
☐ Spacer sleeves, star washer, washer, nut, end cap
☐ (1) 18-gauge light cord with polarized plug
☐ #8 × 1½ in. flathead wood screws
☐ Lamp shade & finial
☐ Wood glue
☐ Finishing materials

Turned Table Lamp

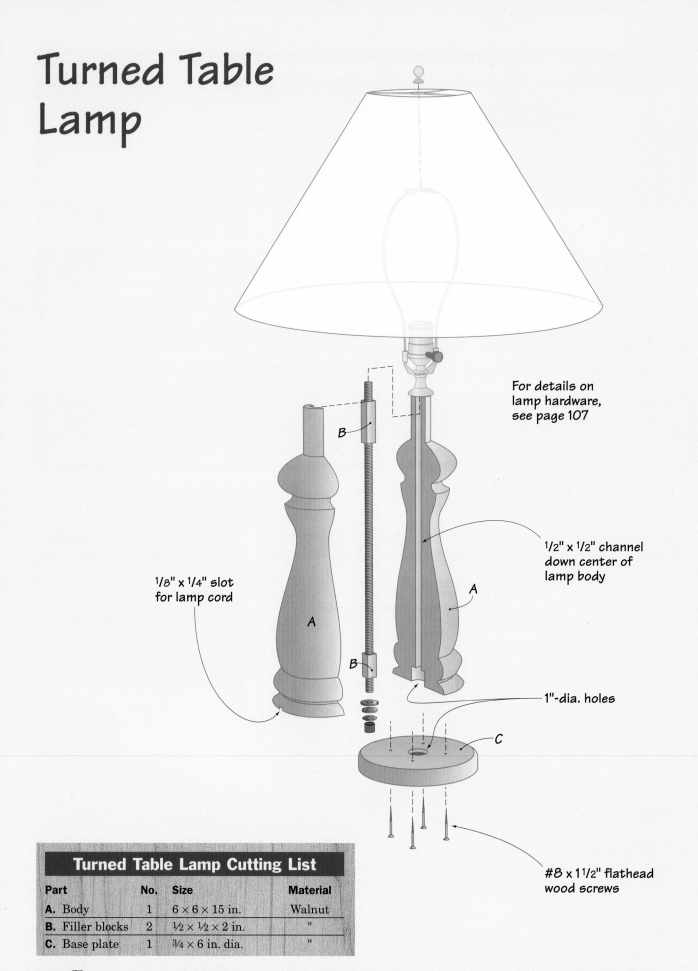

For details on
lamp hardware,
see page 107

$1/2$" x $1/2$" channel
down center of
lamp body

$1/8$" x $1/4$" slot
for lamp cord

A

A

B

B

1"-dia. holes

C

#8 x $11/2$" flathead
wood screws

Turned Table Lamp Cutting List

Part	No.	Size	Material
A. Body	1	$6 \times 6 \times 15$ in.	Walnut
B. Filler blocks	2	$1/2 \times 1/2 \times 2$ in.	"
C. Base plate	1	$3/4 \times 6$ in. dia.	"

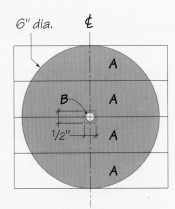

6" dia.

₵

B

A

A

A

A

1/2"

**TOP SECTION VIEW
(Laminated Turning Blank)**

B

A

B

₵

Drill this 1"-dia. x 1"-deep
hole after the lamp
body has been turned

SIDE SECTION VIEW

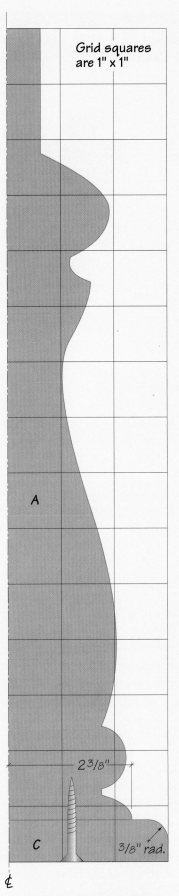

Grid squares
are 1" x 1"

A

2³/₈"

C

3/8" rad.

₵

PROFILE PATTERN

MAKE THE TURNING BLANK

The body of the lamp is turned on a lathe from a turning blank made of strips of ⁶⁄₄ walnut. The blank is constructed by face-gluing the strips together. The two inner strips have mating ¼-in.-deep grooves that form a ½-in.-wide channel when the blank is glued up.

❶ Run a ⁶⁄₄ × 6 in. × 6-ft. walnut board through your jointer to flatten both faces. Try to remove as little material as possible. Cross-cut four 15-in.-long strips (the leftover piece will be used to make the base plate).

❷ Cut a ½-in.-wide, ¼-in.-deep dado down the center of two of the lamp-body boards **(See Photo A)**. When the pieces are joined, these grooves will mate to form the ½-in.-square channel that runs down the middle of the body for the lamp rod and wire. We used a table saw with a dado-blade set, but you could use a router and straight bit or make multiple passes with a standard blade in your table saw.

❸ Cut the two filler blocks for the lamp body to size. The lamp body construction has been simplified by cutting the channel through the body for the wire and rod before gluing the body parts together. The filler blocks will plug the ends of the channel so the blank can be mounted on the lathe. You'll drill through the filler blocks later to open the channel in the lamp body. On a strip of walnut at least 12 in. long, square two adjacent edges on the jointer and carefully rip the other two edges on the table saw to yield a ½ × ½-in. filler strip. The strip should fit snugly into the ½-in.-square channel in the lamp-body boards when you clamp the two boards together. Test the fit of the filler strip and trim the strip if needed, then cross-cut two 2-in. lengths to make the filler blocks.

PHOTO A: Cut a ½-in.-wide × ¼-in.-deep dado down the inner strips for the blank glue-up assembly. Use a featherboard clamped to the saw table to secure the workpieces as you make the cuts.

PHOTO B: Glue and clamp the strips for the blank with the filler blocks glued into the ends of the center channel.

❹ Glue and clamp the lamp body blank together. Apply glue evenly across the mating faces of the four walnut boards, but keep glue out of the center grooves. Glue and insert the filler blocks in the ends of the channels **(See Photo B)**. Apply clamping pressure evenly on two sides of the blank, adjusting the clamps tight enough to close the glue joints but not so tight that you squeeze out the glue.

5 Scrape excess glue squeeze-out off the glued-up blank and joint the laminated edges of the blank flat. Trim the ends of the blank flat on your band saw.

6 Find the center of each blank end by drawing diagonal lines across the blank, connecting opposite corners. Use a compass at these centerpoints to draw 6-in.-dia. circles on the ends. If your blank is less than 6 in. square, draw the largest circle the blank will accommodate.

7 Cut off the corners of the blank. We did this on the band saw. Tilt the band saw table to 45°. Clamp on a tall fence to support the blank as you make the cuts. Set the fence parallel with the miter channel in the saw table so the saw blade just touches the lay-out lines of the circles on the ends of the blank. Trim off the four corners **(See Photo C).** This removes most of the waste, leaving an octagon that will be easier to rough into shape on the lathe.

MOUNT & LAY OUT THE BLANK

8 Mount the lamp blank on the lathe. First, use a mallet to tap the lathe drive center into one of the centers on the end of the blank, forcing the spurs fully into the wood. Mount the blank by inserting the drive center into the lathe headstock, then sliding the tailstock across so the center meets the other end of the blank in the center. Tighten the tailstock on the lathe to hold the blank securely. Adjust the tool rest alongside the blank, at or just below its center. Place the tool rest as close as possible (about ⅛-in. clearance) to the wood, and rotate the blank with the motor off to make sure the tool rest clears the blank. Turn the lathe on at its slowest speed and slowly crank the tailstock hand wheel a little to tighten and seat the tailstock firmly in the blank.

9 Use a large roughing gouge to shape the blank from an octagon into a cylinder. Holding the gouge with the open end of the blade's "U" shape facing upward and the handle angled down, grasp the blade firmly near the handle with one hand and hold the blade steady against the tool rest. *CAUTION: Never let a lathe tool angle downward past horizontal (with the handle higher than the blade) or it can catch on the workpiece and be forced in between the tool rest and the wood.* Bring the gouge's cutting edge slowly into contact with the the wood, and move the tool back and forth along the length of the workpiece in both directions, gradually and evenly removing more and more wood until the edges disappear **(See Photo D).**

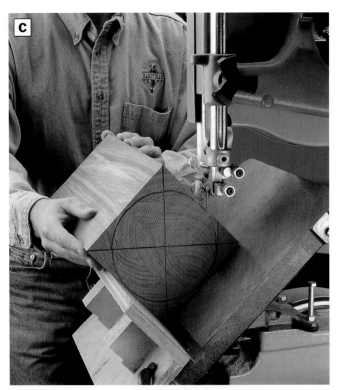

PHOTO C: Trim the corners off the blank, using a band saw. Tip the saw table to 45° and support the workpiece with a fence clamped to the table. Adjust the fence so the blade is aligned with the edge of the circle. Removing these waste pieces will greatly reduce the time needed to rough the blank into a cylinder.

PHOTO D: Rough the blank into a cylinder with a roughing gouge. Hold the gouge firmly in both hands, with the blade resting against the tool rest. Slide the gouge along the tool rest, adjusting the tool rest as necessary, until a smooth and uniform cylinder is achieved.

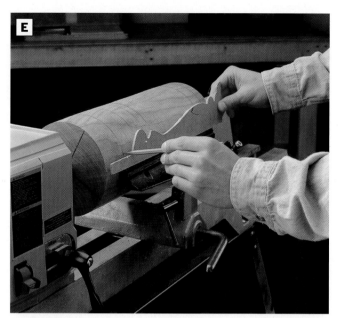

PHOTO E: Transfer reference lines from the half template to the cylinder by applying a pencil as the cylinder spins slowly in the lathe. The reference lines will guide the shaping process.

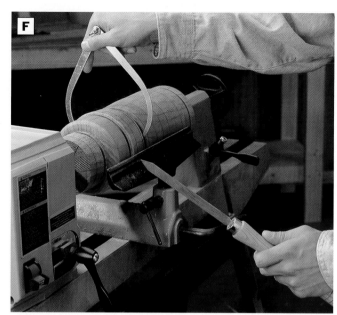

PHOTO F: Rough in the body profile with a parting tool. Check the diameters at the reference points frequently with calipers, to see that they match the diameters you calculated on the template.

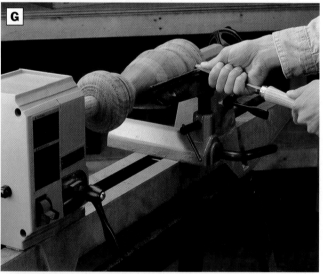

PHOTO G: Use the skew chisel to shape the beads, doing most of the cutting with the heel of the tool. Starting at the top of a bead, tilt the cutting edge down along the required shape in one smooth motion until all the wood is cut away.

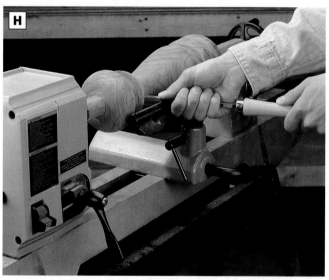

PHOTO H: Use the round-nose scraper to cut coves and for general smoothing. Holding the scraper in a nearly horizontal position produces a scraping, rather than cutting, effect, which is good for smoothing.

Adjust the tool rest as necessary to maintain about ⅛-in. clearance between the edge of the tool rest and the workpiece.

⑩ Make a full-size hardboard template of the *Profile Pattern* on page 101. Cut out the shape with a scroll saw or a coping saw and smooth the edges.

⑪ With the lathe turning slowly, hold the template on the tool rest and against the workpiece. Transfer key profile references (high points, low points and transitions) from the template onto the revolving cylinder with a pencil **(See Photo E).** Make reference marks about every inch along the blank. The result should be a series of layout lines to help reference transition points during the shaping process.

⑫ Use the parting tool to lay out the varying diameters of the body shape. To do this, measure off the template at points that correspond with the reference lines on the lamp-body blank. Double the measurements to get the diameter setting at these spots.

Increase the lathe speed and slowly feed the parting tool (holding it as you did the gouge) into the wood at the first layout line. As you continue to cut deeper, you can lower the handle to raise the blade a bit so it cuts more like a chisel. Shut off the lathe and check your depth of cut frequently with a calipers until you reach the correct diameters **(See Photo F).** Repeat the parting cuts along the blank at each layout line.

SHAPE THE LAMP PROFILE

⓭ Rough in the basic contours of the lamp body with a roughing gouge. Then use a skew chisel to define the shapes at the top and bottom of the lamp body **(See Photo G).** Here's the process for cutting the basic contours:

"V" near the bottom of the lamp: Hold the skew on edge with the heel (the shorter side) down. Feed the blade into the stock at the center of the "V," using the tool rest as a pivot point for the skew.

Beads (tight, convex curves near lamp bottom): Start in the center of each bead (at its high point) with the skew on its side. Turn the tool in an arc as you shave down one side of the bead, cutting with the heel of the skew, until you finish at the base of the bead with the skew on edge. Then cut the other bead curve similarly.

Coves (concave curves): Use a round-nose scraping tool to shape the coves by holding the tool nearly horizontal and swinging it from side to side, pivoting on the tool rest.

Straight shaft at the top: Set the skew on its side at an angle to the workpiece, making a shearing cut along the upper portion of the blank, first in one direction, then back in the other.

⓮ Once the basic shape is cut, increase the lathe speed and smooth off the surfaces of the lamp body with a round-nosed scraper **(See Photo H).**

⓯ Sand the lamp body as it turns slowly on the lathe. Move the tool rest out of the way. Start sanding with 120-grit sandpaper. Then use 150-, and finally 180-grit. Use a light touch when sanding, and hold the sandpaper on the bottom side of the workpiece as it turns. *TIP: Wrap sandpaper around a pad of steel wool to create a flexible sanding pad, which is helpful when sanding into the crevices. Another good trick is to use strips of a belt sander belt to smooth*

PHOTO I: With the lathe turned off, finish-sand the body to remove the circular cross-grain scratches left by sanding with the body spinning.

PHOTO J: Drill a 1-in.-dia hole 1 in. deep through the bottom of the lamp body in the center. Then drill a series of ⅛-in.-deep holes from the edge of the center hole to the edge of the lamp body with a ¼-in. Forstner bit. Clean up the shallow holes with a chisel to create a channel for the lamp cord.

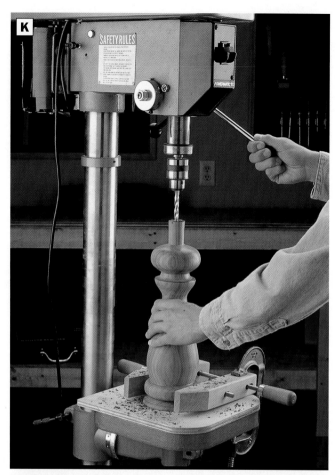

PHOTO K: Drill holes through the filler blocks. Center the lamp body on the drill bit, then clamp it firmly to the drill press table.

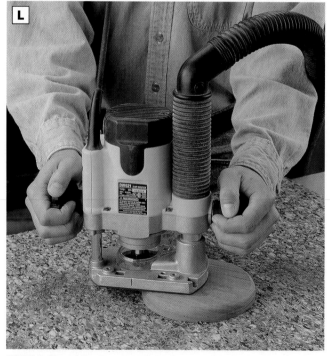

PHOTO L: Round the top edge of the lamp base with a router and a ⅜-in. roundover bit. NOTE: *We used a high-friction router pad to hold the workpiece in place without clamps.*

the workpiece. Again, hold the sanding belt against the bottom side of the spinning workpiece.

16 Turn the lathe off and finish-sand with the grain, using 220-grit sandpaper **(See Photo I).** Sand out all the cross-grain scratches.

DRILL OUT THE ENDS & MAKE THE BASE PLATE

17 Remove the lamp body from the lathe and drill holes to open the cord channel. Clamp the lamp upside-down on the drill press table. Drill a 1-in.-dia. hole, 1 in. deep into the bottom of the lamp in the center, using a Forstner bit. This hole makes a recess for the washers and nut that will hold the lamp hardware in place.

18 Install a ¼-in.-dia. Forstner bit in the drill press and drill a series of ⅛-in.-deep holes from the edge of the center hole in a straight line out to the edge of the lamp body. Clean up the holes with a wood chisel to create a channel for the lamp cord **(See Photo J).**

19 To open the center channel from end to end, drill ½-in.-dia. holes through both filler blocks with the lamp body clamped in place on the drill press **(See Photo K).**

20 Cut a ¾-in.-thick by 6-in.-square piece of walnut from the leftover stock to make the base plate. Use a compass to lay out a 6-in.-dia. circle on the wood. Cut out the circle on a band saw or scroll saw and sand the circle smooth. Use a router with a ⅜-in.-radius roundover bit to shape the top edge of the base plate **(See Photo L).** Finish-sand the base plate.

21 Apply the finish of your choice to the lamp body and base. We wiped on three coats of tung oil with a soft cloth.

WIRE THE LAMP & ATTACH THE BASE PLATE

22 Assemble and wire the lamp hardware (See *Lamp Hardware Anatomy,* page 107). Attach the light socket and lamp harp to a length of hollow threaded pipe that is longer than needed for the lamp. Slide the threaded pipe down into the center channel of the lamp body and mark it for length. *NOTE: Be sure to leave enough pipe at the bottom of the lamp body to attach it with a washer, nut and end cap* **(See Photo M).** Cut the threaded pipe to length with a hacksaw and remove any metal burrs with a metal file. Fasten the lamp light socket and pipe assembly to the lamp body with a flat washer, star washer, nut and end

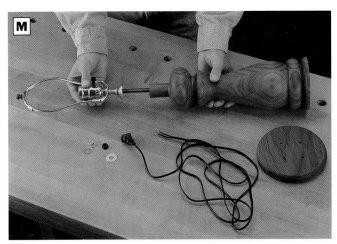

PHOTO M: Attach the light socket to the threaded rod and insert the rod into the lamp body. Mark the rod for length and cut it to size.

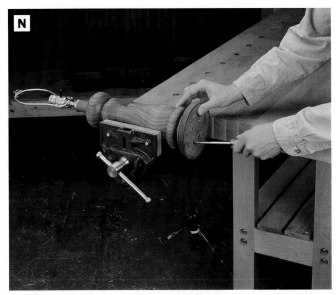

PHOTO N: Feed the cord aside into the groove in the bottom of the lamp body, and screw the lamp base to the body. We clamped the lamp lightly in the bench vise to allow two hands to do this.

cap. Remove the lamp light socket. Thread the lamp cord through the lamp body and connect the lamp cord wires to the socket contact screws. Reinstall the socket on the lamp.

㉓ Attach the base plate to the lamp. Clamp the lamp in a vise and center the base plate on the lamp body. Mark the base plate and drill countersunk pilot holes for four #8 × 1½-in. flathead wood screws, being careful to position the pilot holes clear of the lamp cord. Lay the cord into its channel in the lamp body and drive in the screws to attach the base (**See Photo N**). Remove the lamp from the vise. Stand the lamp upright, place the shade on the top of the harp, and secure the lamp shade to the harp with a threaded finial.

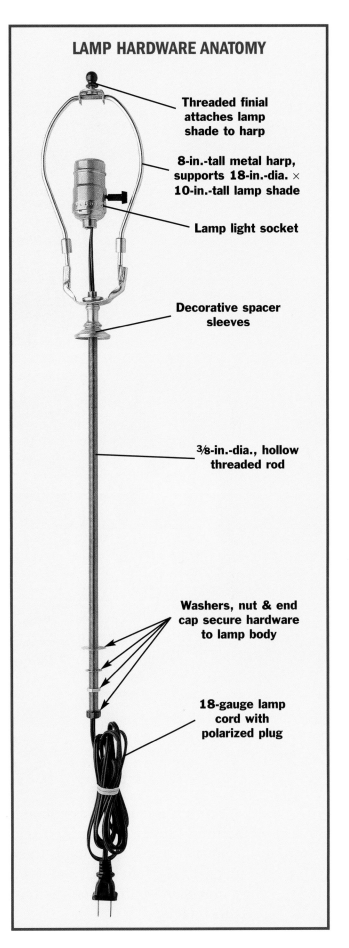

LAMP HARDWARE ANATOMY

Threaded finial attaches lamp shade to harp

8-in.-tall metal harp, supports 18-in.-dia. × 10-in.-tall lamp shade

Lamp light socket

Decorative spacer sleeves

⅜-in.-dia., hollow threaded rod

Washers, nut & end cap secure hardware to lamp body

18-gauge lamp cord with polarized plug

Country Spice Cabinet

Store spices and save valuable cabinet shelf space when you build this wall-mounted spice cabinet. Knotty pine adds to its country styling and makes this project easy on your woodworking budget, too. Four fixed shelves are concealed behind a frame-and-panel door. Contours on the top and bottom make mounting the chest a snap.

Vital Statistics: Country Spice Cabinet

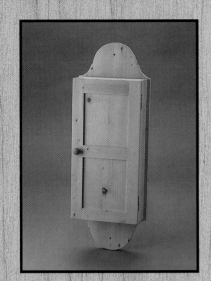

TYPE: Spice cabinet

OVERALL SIZE: 13W by 36H by 5½D

MATERIAL: Pine

JOINERY: Cabinet top and bottom attach to sides with rabbet joints; shelves sit in dadoes cut in sides. Frame-and-panel door rails attach to door stiles with tenons

CONSTRUCTION DETAILS:
· Template used to mark decorative profiles on back panel
· Frame-and-panel door enhances casual, country styling
· Back panel is edge-glued from narrower stock

FINISHING OPTIONS: Orange shellac or color-wash with paint

Building time

PREPARING STOCK
1-2 hours

LAYOUT
2-3 hours

CUTTING PARTS
2-4 hours

ASSEMBLY
2-3 hours

FINISHING
1-2 hours

TOTAL: 8-14 hours

Tools you'll use

· Table saw with dado-blade set
· Jointer
· Bar or pipe clamps
· Jig saw or band saw
· Drill/driver
· Combination square
· Marking knife or utility knife
· Wood chisels

Shopping list

- [ ] (1) ¾ × 9¼ in. × 8 ft. knotty pine (nominal 1 × 10)
- [ ] (1) ¾ × 5½ in. × 8 ft. knotty pine (nominal 1 × 6)
- [ ] (1) ¾ × 2½ in. × 2 ft. knotty pine (nominal 1 × 3)
- [ ] (1) ¼ in. × 2 ft. × 2 ft. knotty pine plywood
- [ ] (2) 2 × 1⅜ in. solid brass ball tip hinges
- [ ] (1) Magnetic door catch
- [ ] #8 × 1½ in. flathead wood screws
- [ ] #8 × 2½ in. brass flathead wood screws
- [ ] Doorknob
- [ ] Glue & finishing materials

Country Spice Cabinet

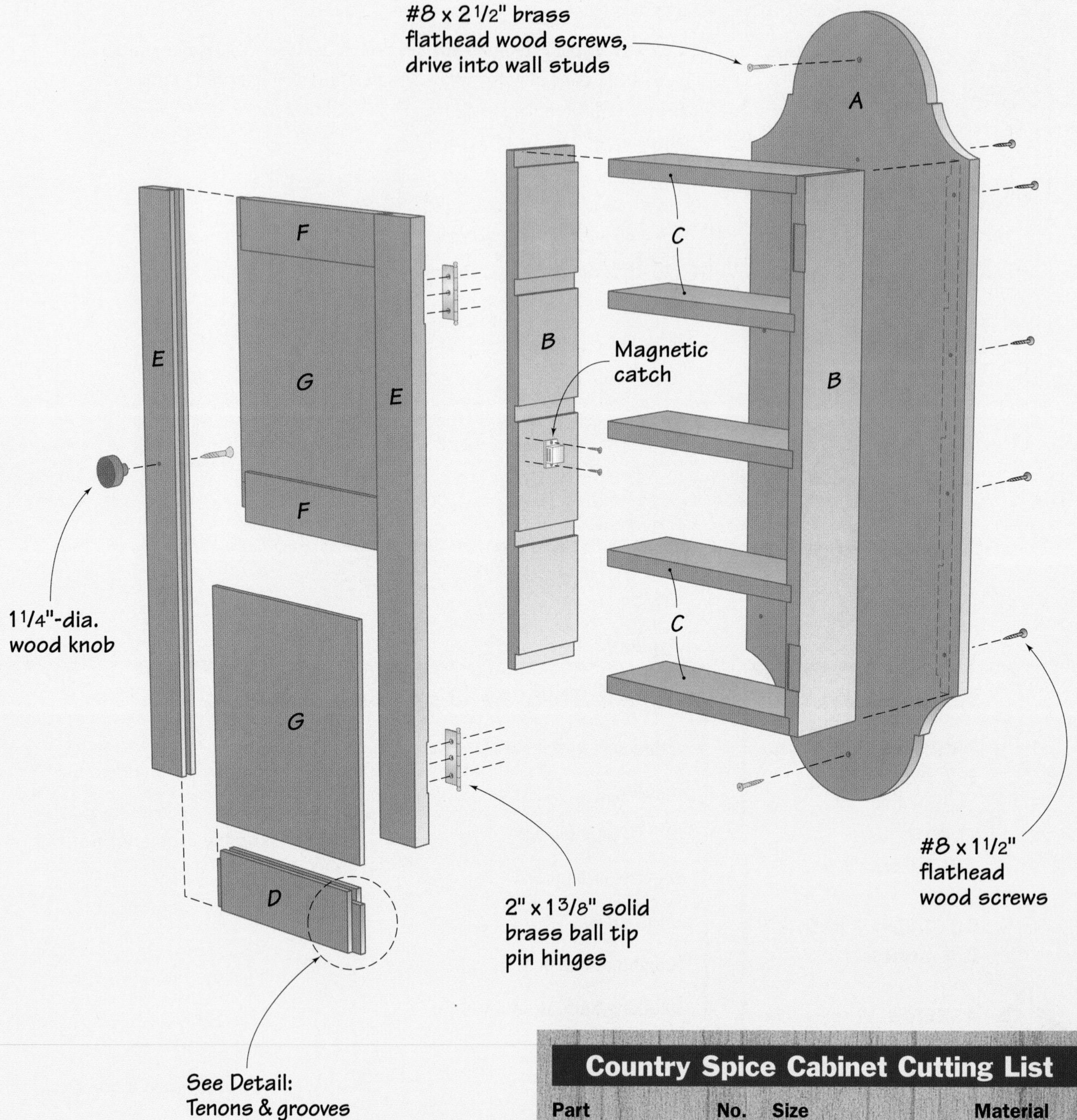

#8 x 2 1/2" brass flathead wood screws, drive into wall studs
A
F
C
E
B
Magnetic catch
G
E
B
F
1 1/4"-dia. wood knob
C
G
D
#8 x 1 1/2" flathead wood screws
2" x 1 3/8" solid brass ball tip pin hinges
See Detail: Tenons & grooves

Country Spice Cabinet Cutting List

Part	No.	Size	Material
A. Back	1	¾ × 13 × 36 in.	Pine
B. Sides	2	¾ × 4 × 24 in.	"
C. Top, Bottom, Shelves	5	¾ × 4 × 11 in.	"
D. Lower rail	1	¾ × 2½ × 9 in.	"
E. Door stiles	2	¾ × 2 × 24 in.	"
F. Center, upper rails	2	¾ × 2 × 9 in.	"
G. Door panels	2	¼ × 8⅞ × 9⅝ in.	Pine plywood

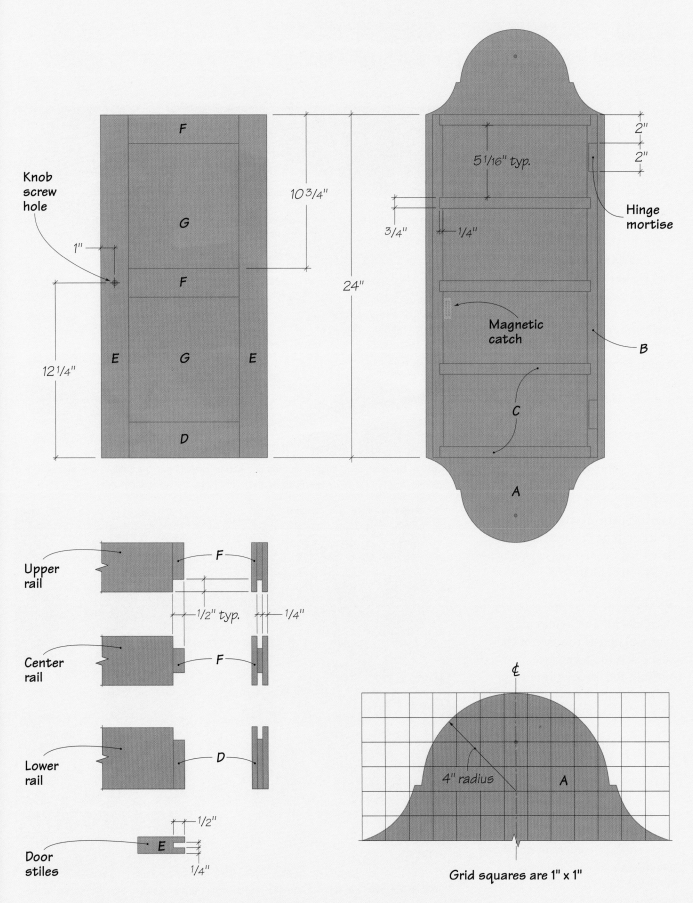

Knob screw hole

F

1"

G

F

E   G   E

D

10 3/4"

12 1/4"

24"

5 1/16" typ.

3/4"   1/4"

2"

2"

Hinge mortise

Magnetic catch

B

C

A

Upper rail

Center rail

Lower rail

Door stiles

F

1/2" typ.   1/4"

F

D

E

1/2"

1/4"

₵

4" radius

A

Grid squares are 1" x 1"

DETAIL: TENONS & GROOVES

Country Spice Cabinet: Step-by-step

MAKE THE CABINET

The casual styling of this spice cabinet combined with our choice of knotty pine lumber makes it a perfect accent piece for a country-style kitchen. Knotty pine is also a good pick if you're building this cabinet on a budget—pine is economical. However, hardwoods like oak, cherry or maple would also be fine choices for this project.

1 Edge-joint and rip one piece of ¾-in.-thick pine to 8½ in. wide and cross-cut it to 24 in. long. This board constitutes both side pieces, which will be dadoed and rabbeted for the shelves as one board and then split in two.

2 Mark the ends of the board for ¼-in.-deep, ¾-in.-wide rabbets that run across the face of the board. On the same face, mark outlines for three ¼-in.-deep, ¾-in.-wide dadoes that are spaced 5¹⁄₁₆ in. apart across the width. Cut the three dado grooves first and then cut both rabbets, using the miter gauge to support the workpiece as you cut (**See Photo A**). We used a dado-blade set in the table saw to cut the dadoes and rabbets. *NOTE: When cutting these rabbets, attach an auxiliary wood fence to your saw fence to keep the dado blade from damaging your metal fence.*

PHOTO A: Gang-cut shelf dadoes and top and bottom rabbets into the cabinet side pieces with a dado-blade set in the table saw. Then rip the board to create two cabinet sides.

PHOTO B: Assemble the cabinet with glue and clamps. The shelves slide into the dadoes in the side panels, and the top and bottom pieces sit in the rabbets. Use scrap-wood cauls between the clamp jaws and the cabinet side panels.

3 Rip the board into two 4-in.-wide pieces to create the sides.

4 Rip and cross-cut five ¾-in.-thick pieces to 4 in. × 11 in. to make the top, bottom and three shelves. Finish-sand the shelves and the interior faces of the top, bottom and sides.

5 Assemble the cabinet. Spread wood glue in the dadoes and rabbets of each side and insert the shelves, top and bottom into the grooves. Clamp up the cabinet with wood cauls between the clamp jaws and the cabinet pieces, and make sure the assembly is square **(See Photo B).** Do this by measuring the carcase from corner to corner. When the measurements are the same, the carcase is square. Adjust by repositioning the clamps and retightening. Wipe away any glue squeeze-out with a damp rag before the glue dries.

MAKE & ATTACH THE BACK

6 Rip four ¾-in.-thick boards to 3½ in. wide, then cross-cut them to 36¼ in. long. Flatten the long edges of each board on a jointer and edge-glue the boards together into one wide panel. You can use biscuits to help align the boards if you like, but glue alone is sufficient for strength. When the glue has dried, scrape and sand the back panel flat and smooth, then rip it to 13 in. wide.

7 Make a paper or posterboard template of the rounded profile for the top and bottom of the back panel, using the grid drawing on page 111. Use spray adhesive or double-sided tape to mount the template to ¼-in.-thick hardboard scrap. Cut the template to shape with a jig saw or band saw and smooth the cut surfaces of the template with a file.

PHOTO C: Use a template to transfer the profile shape onto the top and bottom of the back panel. Cut out the shape with a jig saw or band saw and smooth the edges with sandpaper.

PHOTO D: Center the cabinet on the back panel and mark the cabinet outline onto the panel. Flip the back panel over and realign the cabinet and back panel again. Use the cabinet outline as a reference to screw the two parts together. Drill a pilot hole before driving each screw.

PHOTO E: Cut a ¼-in.-wide, ½-in.-deep dado groove in one long edge of the door stiles and top and bottom rails for the door panels. Cut a dado on each long edge of the center rail. Use a featherboard and pushstick to hold each workpiece firmly against the saw table and fence.

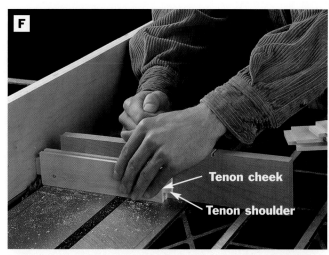

PHOTO F: Cut the tenons on the rail ends. The cheek cuts should be made first with the workpieces lying flat on the saw table. Then raise the blades and tip the boards on their sides to cut the shoulders.

PHOTO G: Apply finish to the door panels. In order to finish both sides without waiting for one side to dry first, we made a quick drying rack from scrap plywood with screw tips facing up. After finishing one side of both panels we held them by the edges and flipped them over, setting the still-wet sides down on the screw tips. The screw tips provide support without marring the finish as it dries.

PHOTO H: Assemble the door rails, stiles and panels together to check the fit. Disassemble the parts and apply glue to the tenons. Reassemble the parts, using clamps to press the joints together.

8 Trace the template onto the top and bottom of the back panel so the overall length of the back panel is 36 in. Cut along your layout lines with a jig saw or band saw **(See Photo C).** Sand the edges and faces of the back panel smooth, and finish-sand the outsides of the carcase.

9 Lay the back panel on a flat surface and place the cabinet on top of it. Orient the cabinet so that the back panel overhangs it by ½ in. along both long edges, and center the cabinet top-to-bottom on the back panel. Mark the cabinet and shelf outlines onto the back panel with a pencil, then flip the back panel so the outlines will show on the back of the spice cabinet when it is done. Reorient the back panel on the cabinet and use the cabinet outlines as reference marks for attaching the back panel to the cabinet using eight #8 × 1½-in.-long wood screws **(See Photo D).**

MAKE THE DOOR

10 Cut two 8⅞-in.-wide by 9⅝-in.-long door panels from ¼-in.-thick knotty pine plywood. *NOTE: We used plywood instead of solid pine stock to avoid needing to resaw the wide board to ¼ in.* If this plywood is not available in your area, you could also substitute birch plywood of the same thickness. Finish-sand the door panels on both sides.

11 Rip-cut and cross-cut the two door stiles and three door rails to size. Straighten the long edges on a jointer and be sure the ends of each workpiece are square.

12 Install a dado-blade set in the table saw, and set its width to ¼ in. and height above the saw table to ½ in. Set the saw's fence ¼ in. away from the blade. Cut grooves in one long edge of each stile and the upper and lower rails. Cut grooves in both long edges of the center rail **(See Photo E).**

13 Reset the width of the dado blade to ½ in. and height to ¼ in. Set each rail with its face on the saw table and cut tenons on both ends (See *Detail: Tenons & Grooves,* page 111). Then raise the dado blade to ½ in. and cut the shoulders into the grooved edge of the top and bottom rails. Cut shoulders into both edges of the center rail on both ends **(See Photo F).** Sand the rails and stiles smooth.

14 Apply a coat of finish to both sides of the door panels **(See Photo G).** Do this now, because once the door is assembled, the edges of the door panels will be inaccessible within the rail and stile grooves.

15 Apply glue to the rail tenons and to the portion of the grooves where the tenons will seat. Fit the door panels, rails and stiles together and clamp up the door **(See Photo H).** Check the door for square by measuring the diagonals.

ATTACH THE DOOR & HARDWARE

16 Shim the door with scrap strips so it sits beside the cabinet with its wider lower rail at the bottom of the cabinet. Set the hinges in place on the door and the cabinet edge, 2 in. from the top and bottom of the cabinet. Allow clearance for the door hinge knuckles. Drill pilot holes and install a few screws to hold each hinge in place. Use a sharp marking knife to score the hinge outline onto the wood **(See Photo I).** Chisel out the hinge mortises to the depth of the hinge leaves.

17 Install the hinges **(See Photo J).** Adjust the hinges as needed so the door hangs squarely on the cabinet and closes properly.

18 Drill a knob hole through the door stile opposite the hinge side, 12¼ in. from the cabinet bottom and centered on the stile width. Install the knob.

19 Mount the magnetic catch on the inside face of the left cabinet side panel. Install the strike plate on the inside of the door. Adjust the catch forward or backward so it catches properly.

FINISHING TOUCHES

20 Drill countersunk pilot holes, one at the top of the back panel and one at the bottom, as shown

PHOTO I: Score the outlines of the hinges onto the cabinet edge and the door with a sharp marking knife. We drilled pilot holes and put a few screws into the hinges to keep them from moving.

PHOTO J: Hang the door, using a scrap block to hold the door in place. Drill centered pilot holes and drive screws to mount the hinges. Take care not to overtighten the screws, as they can strip out easily in the soft pine.

in the illustration on page 110. The spice cabinet is attached to the wall with screws driven through these holes.

21 Apply a topcoat to all exposed surfaces of the spice cabinet. We used orange shellac, the traditional finish for knotty pine.

Jewelry Box

Add this jewelry box to your list of must-build projects for gift giving, and surprise a special person in your life. Our compact maple jewelry box features walnut accents to highlight the beauty of contrasting wood tones and features a removable tray with compartments to store many precious trinkets and jewelry. The raised-panel lid and tapered feet and handle give the design a clean, contemporary look.

Vital Statistics: Jewelry Box

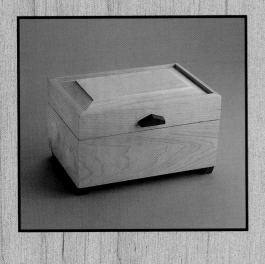

TYPE: Jewelry box

OVERALL SIZE: 12W by 7H by 8D

MATERIAL: Maple

JOINERY: Miter, dado, rabbet joints

CONSTRUCTION DETAILS:

· Corner grain matches all around box sides
· Raised-panel lid
· Tray rests on the top edges of tray supports. When lid is opened, tray protrudes above box and can be lifted out
· Divided tray compartment
· Walnut feet and handle details

FINISHING OPTIONS: A clear finish, like Danish oil or varnish, is recommended to bring out depth of the maple wood grain, particularly if curly maple stock is used

Building time

 PREPARING STOCK
2-3 hours

 LAYOUT
2-3 hours

 CUTTING PARTS
2-4 hours

 ASSEMBLY
2-3 hours

 FINISHING
1-2 hours

TOTAL: 9-15 hours

Tools you'll use

· Jointer
· Planer
· Router table with auxiliary fence and featherboard
· Raised-panel router bit
· Band saw
· Table saw
· Dado-blade set
· Bar clamps
· Spring clamps
· Sanding station
· Wood chisels
· Combination square

Shopping list

☐ (1) 6/4 × 6½ in. × 2 ft. maple

☐ (1) 3/4 × 8 in. × 4 ft. maple

☐ (1) ¼ in. × 2 ft. × 2 ft. maple or birch plywood

☐ 1 × 1 in. × 2 ft. walnut scrap

☐ (2) 95° solid-brass jewelry box hinges

☐ Wood glue

☐ 3/4-, ½-in. brads

☐ Wide masking tape or plastic packing tape

☐ Finishing materials

Jewelry Box

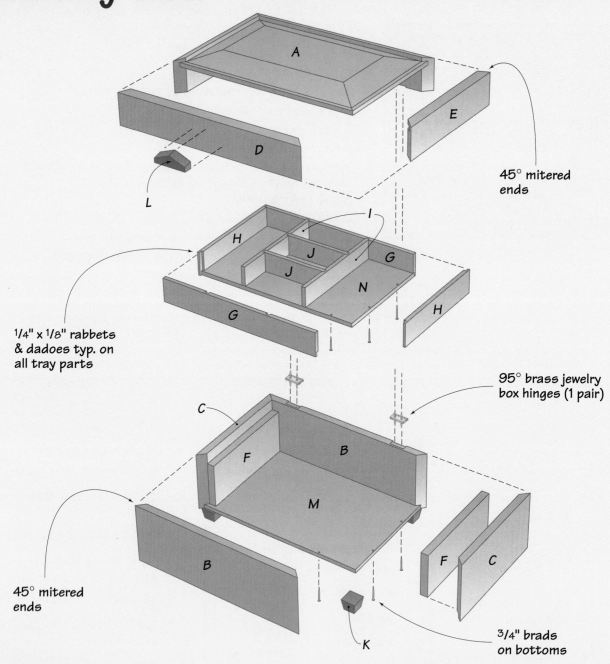

45° mitered ends

1/4" x 1/8" rabbets & dadoes typ. on all tray parts

95° brass jewelry box hinges (1 pair)

45° mitered ends

3/4" brads on bottoms

Jewelry Box Cutting List

Part	No.	Size	Material		Part	No.	Size	Material
A. Lid	1	3/4 × 7 3/8 × 11 1/2 in.	Maple		**H.** Tray ends	2	1/4 × 1 1/2 × 6 7/8 in.	Maple
B. Box sides	2	1/2 × 4 × 12 in.	"		**I.** Tray dividers	2	1/4 × 1 1/4 × 6 5/8 in.	"
C. Box ends	2	1/2 × 4 × 8 in.	"		**J.** Tray dividers	2	1/4 × 1 1/4 × 4 1/4 in.	"
D. Lid sides	2	1/2 × 2 × 12 in.	"		**K.** Feet	4	1 × 1 × 3/4 in.	Walnut
E. Lid ends	2	1/2 × 2 × 8 in.	"		**L.** Handle	1	1/2 × 2 × 3/4 in.	"
F. Tray supports	2	1/2 × 3 × 7 in.	"		**M.** Box bottom	1	1/4 × 7 1/2 × 11 1/2 in.	Maple plywood
G. Tray sides	2	1/4 × 1 1/2 × 10 5/8 in.	"		**N.** Tray bottom	1	1/4 × 6 5/8 × 10 5/8 in.	"

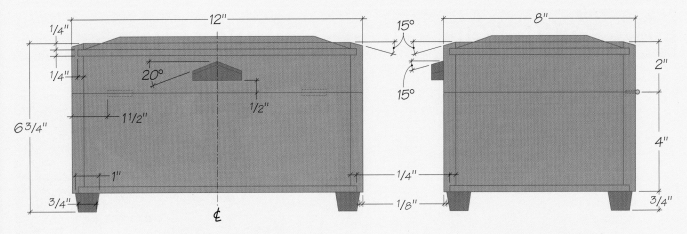

FRONT SECTION

SIDE SECTION

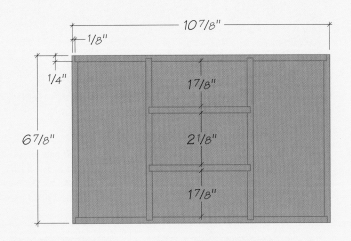

TRAY TOP VIEW

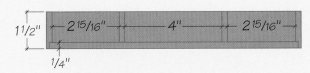

TRAY FRONT SECTION

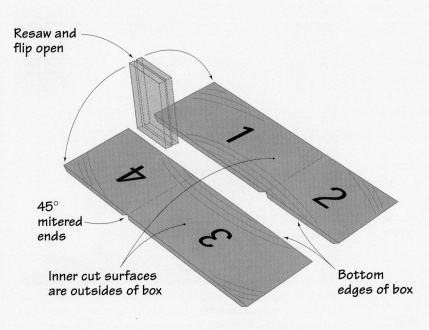

Resaw and
flip open

45°
mitered
ends

Inner cut surfaces
are outsides of box

Bottom
edges of box

RESAW TO MATCH GRAIN

Cut top bevel and
lid panel groove
before assembly

Grain is
matched at
all corners

ASSEMBLED BOX

MAKE AND ASSEMBLE THE BOX

The box and lid sides and ends are resawn and cut from one piece of maple to give a four-corner grain match (two sides have continuous grain and two are butt- or end-matched). A prominent grain pattern will show off the four-way match better than an all-over pattern like bird's-eye, but a bit of figure or curl to the wood will add a richness that is welcome in just about any woodworking project.

1 Cut the lid panel to size, according to the dimensions given in the *Cutting List,* page 118.

2 Install a vertical-style panel raising router bit in the router table. Fasten a tall auxiliary fence to the router table. If you have an adjustable-speed router, set the speed to about 13,000 rpm. Using a featherboard to secure the lid panel, rout the shape, removing about ⅛ in. of material with each pass until you reach the desired profile. The finished panel should have a ¼ × ¼-in. lip around the edge that will fit into the groove in the lid **(See Photo A).** NOTE: *Using a panel raising bit in a router table is an easy and safe way to cut a raised panel. The tall auxiliary fence provides a secure bearing surface for the panel, and the featherboard keeps the panel tight against the fence as it passes the cutter.*

3 Plane the 6/4 stock for the box sides and ends to 1¼ in. thick. Joint one long edge and rip the stock to 6¼ in., then cross-cut to 21 in. in length. (This piece comprises the box sides and ends and the lid sides and ends, which will be cut apart later after the box is assembled.)

4 Mark a centerline along the ripped edge, dividing the board in two. With the jointed edge riding on the saw table, resaw the board on a band saw **(See Photo B).** Use a resaw jig to guide the workpiece.

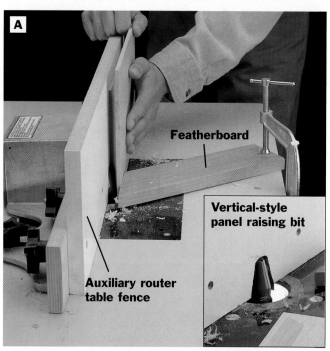

PHOTO A: Rout the raised-panel face of the lid, taking off only about ⅛ in. at a time. Do this by starting with the router fence nearly flush to the edge of the bit, and move the fence further into the bit for each pass. Removing too much material in one pass could burn the lid panel or prematurely dull the router bit.

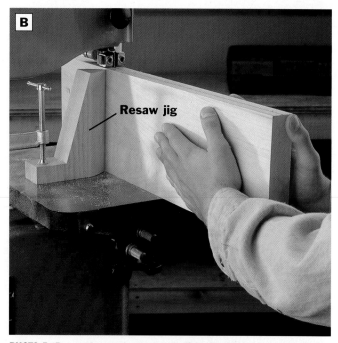

PHOTO B: Resaw the maple stock in half for the sides and ends of the box, using a marked centerline as a guide for the blade. A shop-made resaw jig clamped to the saw table will help square the board to the table and keep the blade tracking along the cutting line.

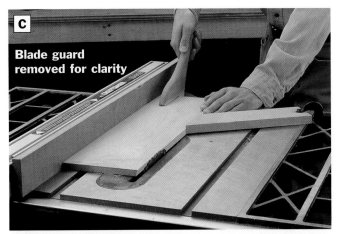

PHOTO C: Cut a 15° bevel into the top edges of the two resawn box boards. Use a featherboard and pushstick for accuracy and safety.

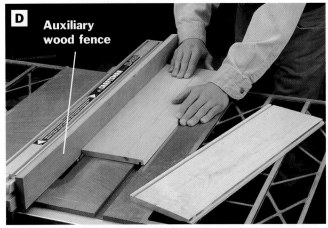

PHOTO D: Cut the bottom rabbet into the lower edge of the box sides. Attach an auxiliary wood fence if you use a table saw and dado-blade set to cut these rabbets.

PHOTO E: Cut the sides to length on the table saw, mitering the ends at the same time. Use a miter gauge set to exactly 90° to feed the stock through the blade.

PHOTO F: Apply glue to the mitered faces and use tape to hold the corner joints together while the glue sets. Tack the box bottom panel into its rabbet. The lid panel dado gets no glue.

5 Plane the two resawn board halves to ½ in. thick. It is important to label the four lid and four box parts on the two boards at this point. Use the illustrations on the bottom of page 119 as a guide.

6 Set your table saw blade to 15° and cut a bevel on the lid edges of both resawn workpieces **(See Photo C).**

7 Cut a ¼ × ¼-in. dado along the edge of both resawn boards, ¼ in. down from the top of the beveled edge. Then cut a ¼-in.-deep rabbet for the box bottom along the opposite long edge of each board **(See Photo D).** To do this, first fasten an auxiliary wood fence to the saw fence to keep the dado blade from damaging the metal fence.

8 Install a combination table saw blade and tilt it to 45°. Test the angle cut on some scrap stock to be sure

it is exact. Then use a miter gauge to feed the workpieces as you cut the four sides to length, with a 45° miter at each end **(See Photo E).**

9 Cut the plywood bottom to size. Set the bottom panel into the rabbets on the box ends and sides, and the lid panel in the groove near the bevel. Check the fit of the mitered corners. NOTE: *The lid panel is narrower than the bottom panel to allow the lid to expand across the grain.* Disassemble the box, and sand the inside faces of all the parts, as well as the top surface of the lid panel.

10 Arrange the box side and end pieces end-to-end, with their outside faces up and the grain aligned. With the mitered edges pressed tightly together, run a strip of wide masking tape or clear plastic packing tape along each of the three corner joints and burnish it. Flip the assembly over and spread wood glue

PHOTO G: Apply bar clamps across the box length and width to ensure tight miter joints. Wood cauls between the box and the clamp jaws will help distribute clamping pressure.

PHOTO H: Rip the box and lid into two pieces on the table saw, with the box bottom against the saw fence. Raise the blade to ⅝ in. and cut one end, then cut adjacent sides, working your way around the box.

PHOTO I: Glue the tray supports to the inside ends of the box. Butt them against the box bottom and hold them tight with spring clamps.

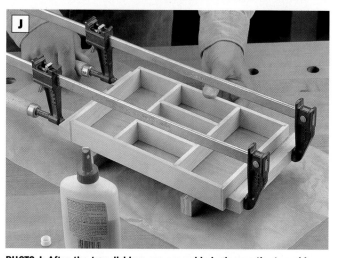

PHOTO J: After the tray dividers are assembled, glue up the tray sides and ends and tack the tray bottom in place with brads.

into both members of each miter joint (use no glue for the lid or bottom panels to allow for wood movement). Roll the assembly into a box with the bottom panel and lid in place, and tape the last joint closed **(See Photo F).**

11 Use bar clamps clamped across the width and length of the jewelry box to further close the miters **(See Photo G).** Allow the glue to dry, remove the clamps and tack the bottom panel into the rabbet with ¾-in. brads.

12 Remove the tape, working carefully to avoid tearing away the wood grain at the corners. If it's difficult to do this, soften the adhesive with a heat gun. Apply mineral spirits with a rag to remove any tape adhesive residue.

13 With the box bottom against the table saw fence, rip the lid from the box, starting on an end and cutting clockwise around the box side panels **(See Photo H).** CAUTION: *Be sure to support the lid on the last cut, but be careful not to pinch the blade between the lid and the box as you make the cut, which could cause the saw to kick back.*

14 Cut the two tray supports to size. Sand the inside face and top edge of each support, and glue the supports to the inside faces of the box ends with the lower edges butted against the bottom panel **(See Photo I).**

ASSEMBLE THE TRAY

15 Surface-plane ¾-in. stock down to ¼ in. for the tray parts. Rip- and cross-cut the tray sides, ends, dividers and bottom to size. CAUTION: *Use care when* *cutting these small workpieces to size, especially if you cut them on a table saw. If you make the cuts on a table saw, start with stock that is long enough to keep your hands a safe distance away from the blade.*

16 Cut ¼-in.-wide × ⅛-in.-deep dadoes in the long tray dividers and the tray sides, as shown in the *Tray (Top View)* illustration, page 119. Then, cut ⅛-in.-deep, ¼-in.-wide rabbets in the ends of both tray ends. Cut ⅛-in.-deep, ¼-in.-wide rabbets along the bottom inside edges of the tray ends and sides to accept the tray bottom. Sand all the tray parts smooth with 150- to 180-grit sandpaper.

17 Glue and clamp the center tray divider unit together and let the glue dry. Then glue and clamp the tray sides and ends to the assembled dividers with the divider ends set in the dado grooves (**See Photo J**). Drill pilot holes and use ½-in. brads to fasten the tray bottom in place.

ADD THE HINGES, FEET & HANDLE

18 Cut a 1 × 1 × 12-in. blank of walnut for the jewelry box feet. Cross-cut one end square and mark a line around it, ¾ in. from the end. Starting at this line, bevel the four faces of the foot so they taper to ¾ in. square at the end of the blank. Sand the foot tapers on a stationary disk sander (**See Photo K**), then cut off the foot. Repeat this procedure for the remaining three feet.

19 Cut a piece of walnut to ½ in. thick × ¾ in. wide × 2 in. long for the handle and square the ends. Divide one long edge in half and draw 20° beveled lines from this point to either short end of the handle blank. Cut along these angle lines with a band saw to create a five-sided shape that matches the handle on the *Front View* illustration, page 119. Designate a front face to the handle and bevel the edges from the back face toward the front to give the handle a sleeker profile and mimic the leg tapers.

20 Finish-sand the feet, handle, outsides of the box and tray with 180-grit sandpaper. Because maple is dense and closed-grained, the maple box needs to be sanded with fine paper—220-grit—to remove fine scratches; otherwise they'll show up in the finish. This finishing step is particularly important if you plan to apply a wood stain to the jewelry box.

21 Mark out the hinge leaf mortises on the lid and box, and cut the mortises with a sharp wood chisel.

PHOTO K: For safety and to maintain control over the workpiece, sand the tapers on a long walnut blank, then cut off a foot and repeat for the other three feet.

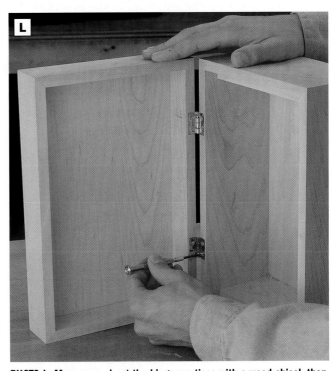

PHOTO L: Measure and cut the hinge mortises with a wood chisel, then install the brass jewelry box hinges to attach the lid to the box.

Install the hinges, drilling pilot holes for the screws first (**See Photo L**).

22 Glue and clamp the feet to the bottom of the box, ⅛ in. in from the corners. Glue and clamp the handle onto the lid (See *Front Section,* page 119).

FINISHING TOUCHES

23 Apply a clear finish to show off the natural beauty of the maple and walnut—we used three coats of Danish oil.

Blanket Chest

Build this contemporary-styled blanket chest as a gift for an upcoming wedding, and you'll surely win a special place in the heart of the bride-to-be. Our spacious design includes a large open storage compartment accessible by way of a tip-up lid, as well as a deep drawer underneath. We built the chest mostly from solid poplar, but you could build the project entirely from hardwood plywood as well.

Vital Statistics: Blanket Chest

TYPE: Blanket chest

OVERALL SIZE: 19½D by 37½W by 29H

MATERIAL: Poplar, hardwood plywood

JOINERY: Rabbet, butt, dado, double-dado, biscuited miter joints

CONSTRUCTION DETAILS:

· Two-compartment chest. Larger compartment is accessible from top of chest and is separated from bottom drawer compartment

· Double-dado joints and false drawer front

· Drawer rides on wooden runners

· Base features feet that taper in two directions

FINISHING OPTIONS: Outside chest surfaces finished with flat oil-based paint. Inside compartment surfaces and drawer parts topcoated with Danish oil or varnish

Building time

PREPARING STOCK
4-5 hours

LAYOUT
3-4 hours

CUTTING PARTS
3-5 hours

ASSEMBLY
4-6 hours

FINISHING
2-3 hours

TOTAL: 16-23 hours

Tools you'll use

· Jointer

· Planer

· Table saw

· (2) Strap clamps

· Bar or pipe clamps

· Spring clamps

· Jig saw

· Biscuit joiner

· Drill/driver

· Wood chisel

Shopping list

☐ (7) 4/4 × 8 in. × 8 ft. poplar

☐ (3) 4/4 × 6 in. × 8 ft. poplar

☐ (1) 3/4 in. × 4 ft. × 4 ft. birch plywood

☐ (1) 1/4 in. × 2 ft. × 4 ft. birch plywood

☐ #20 biscuits

☐ #8 x 1¼, 1¾ in. flathead wood screws

☐ 1 in. brads

☐ (1) 34½ in. piano hinge and ½ in. brass screws

☐ Wood glue

☐ (2) 1¼-in.-dia. wood knobs

☐ Finishing materials

Blanket Chest

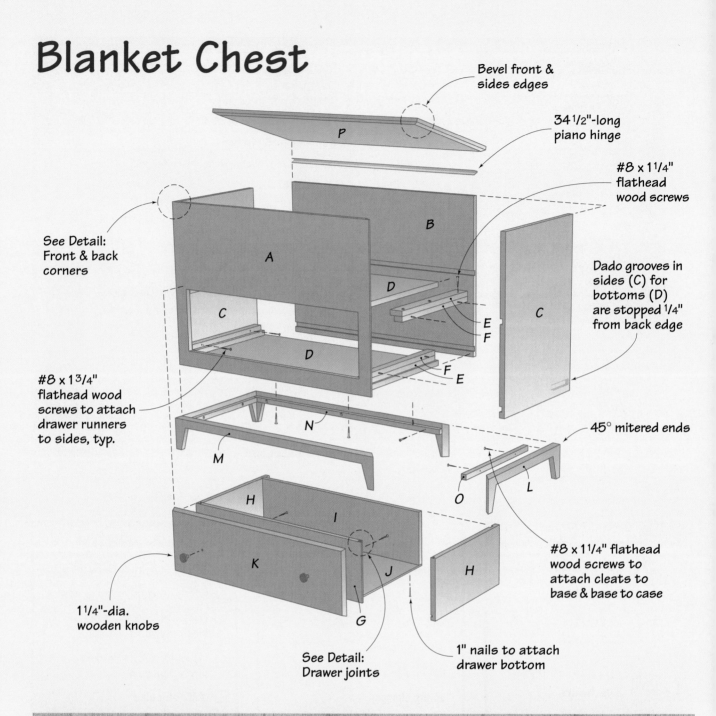

Bevel front & sides edges

34 1/2"-long piano hinge

#8 x 1 1/4" flathead wood screws

See Detail: Front & back corners

Dado grooves in sides (C) for bottoms (D) are stopped 1/4" from back edge

#8 x 1 3/4" flathead wood screws to attach drawer runners to sides, typ.

45° mitered ends

#8 x 1 1/4" flathead wood screws to attach cleats to base & base to case

1 1/4"-dia. wooden knobs

See Detail: Drawer joints

1" nails to attach drawer bottom

A B C D E F G H I J K L M N O P

Blanket Chest Cutting List

Part	No.	Size	Material
A. Front	1	3/4 × 24 × 36 in.	Poplar
B. Back	1	3/4 × 23 7/8 × 34 1/2 in.	"
C. Sides	2	3/4 × 24 × 17 3/4 in.	"
D. Center shelf/ bottom panel	2	3/4 × 17 1/4 × 35 1/4 in.	Plywood
E. Drawer runners	4	3/4 × 2 × 16 1/2 in.	Poplar
F. Drawer guides	4	3/4 × 1 1/4 × 16 1/2 in.	"
G. Drawer front	1	3/4 × 9 × 31 7/8 in.	"

Part	No.	Size	Material
H. Drawer sides	2	3/4 × 9 × 16 3/4 in.	Poplar
I. Drawer back	1	3/4 × 8 1/4 × 31 1/8 in.	"
J. Drawer bottom	1	1/4 × 15 7/8 × 31 1/8 in.	Plywood
K. Drawer face	1	3/4 × 9 3/4 × 32 5/8 in.	Poplar
L. Base ends	2	3/4 × 5 × 19 1/2	"
M. Base sides	2	3/4 × 5 × 37 1/2	"
N. Cleats (side)	2	3/4 × 3/4 × 36	"
O. Cleats (end)	2	3/4 × 3/4 × 16 1/2	"
P. Lid	1	3/4 × 18 3/4 × 37 1/2 in.	"

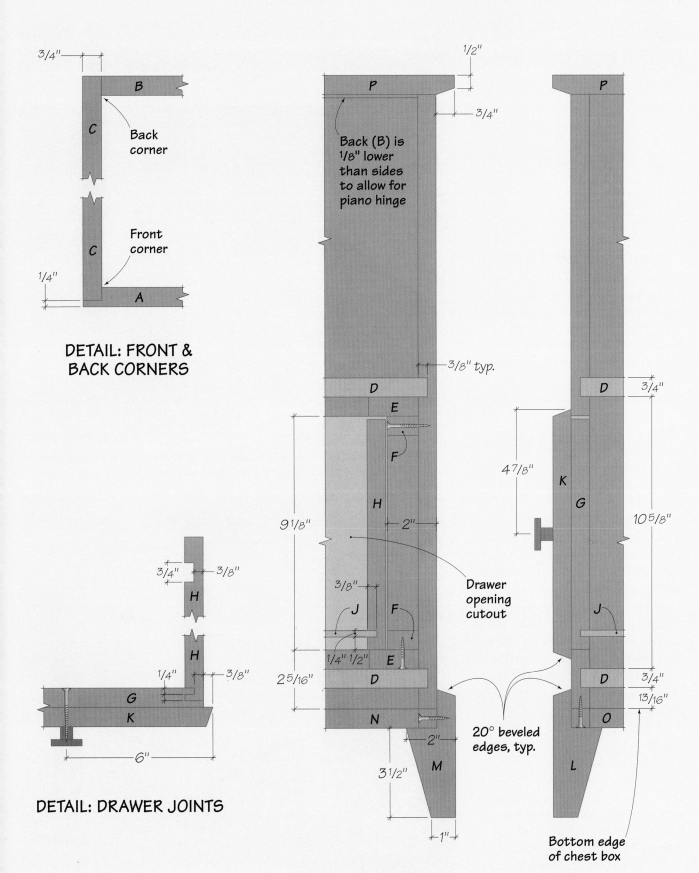

DETAIL: FRONT & BACK CORNERS

3/4"

B

Back corner

C

Front corner

1/4"

C

A

DETAIL: DRAWER JOINTS

3/4"   3/8"

H

3/4"   3/8"

H

1/4"   3/8"

G

K

6"

Back (B) is 1/8" lower than sides to allow for piano hinge

1/2"

P

3/4"

3/8" typ.

D

E

F

H

2"

9 1/8"

3/8"

J

F

1/4" 1/2"

E

2 5/16"

D

N

2"

3 1/2"

M

1"

Drawer opening cutout

20° beveled edges, typ.

P

D

3/4"

4 7/8"

K

G

10 5/8"

J

D

3/4"

13/16"

O

L

Bottom edge of chest box

FRONT SECTION VIEW   **SIDE SECTION VIEW**

ASSEMBLE THE CHEST CARCASE

The front, back and side panels of the blanket chest carcase are made from glued-up panels of solid poplar. We chose poplar because it's durable, less expensive than other hardwood types and has a tight grain pattern that takes a painted finish well.

1 Surface-plane all the poplar boards you plan to use for the blanket chest to ¾ in. thick, and square the long edges on a jointer. Cross-cut enough stock to build glue-up panels for the front, back and sides of the chest carcase. The panel should be about 1 in. longer than their finished length. Orient the boards so the grain direction runs horizontally along all carcase panels. Edge-glue and clamp the panels, alternating clamps above and below the panels to distribute clamping pressure. Once the glue dries, rip- and cross-cut the carcase panels to size. *NOTE: The back panel is ⅛ in. narrower than the front panel to allow clearance for the chest lid hinge.*

2 Cut ¾-in.-wide, ½-in.-deep rabbets along both ends of the blanket chest front panel (**See Photo A**). The carcase side panels will fit into these rabbets. We used a dado-blade set in the table saw to cut the two rabbets, but you could use a router with a piloted

PHOTO A: Cut ¾-in.-wide, ½-in.-deep rabbet joints along the ends of the carcase front panel. Attach an auxiliary wood fence to keep the dado blade from damaging the metal saw fence.

Auxiliary wood fence

PHOTO B: Assemble the carcase, gluing and clamping up the front, back, sides, center shelf and bottom panel. Clamp from both directions, using scrapwood pads between the clamp jaws and the carcase. Measure across the diagonals to check for squareness.

rabbeting bit instead, or a straight bit and straightedge cutting guide. *NOTE: Attach an auxiliary wood fence to your table saw to keep the dado blade from damaging the metal fence.*

3 Cut ¾-in.-wide by ⅜-in.-deep dadoes in the inside faces of the front and back panels. The upper dadoes accept the center shelf. Cut them so the bottom shoulders of the dadoes are 12³⁄₁₆ in. up from the bottom edges of the panels. The lower dadoes accept the bottom panel. Cut them 1³⁄₁₆ in. up from the bottom edges.

4 Rip-cut and cross-cut the center shelf and bottom panels to size from ¾-in.-thick plywood.

5 Cut stopped dadoes in the side panels for the center shelf and bottom panel. The dadoes should start at the front edge of each side panel and stop ⅜ in. before reaching the back edges of the panels. They should be at the same height as the dadoes in the front and back panels. Square up the ends of the stopped dadoes with a sharp wood chisel.

6 Assemble the carcase. Spread glue along the rabbets and dadoes of the carcase parts, then clamp together the front, back, sides, center shelf and bottom panel **(See Photo B).** Make sure the chest carcase is square by measuring diagonally from corner to corner; if the lengths of the diagonals are equal, the carcase is square. Adjust the clamps as needed to square the carcase.

7 On the front of the carcase, lay out the drawer opening so it's 9⅛ in. high by 32 in. long, and centered side-to-side. The bottom of the drawer opening should be 2⁵⁄₁₆

PHOTO C: Use a jig saw to cut out the drawer opening in the carcase front. Run the edge of the jig saw base against a straightedge to keep the cut straight and smooth. Drill ½-in.-dia. starter holes in the corners of the cutout area before sawing.

PHOTO D: Cut a ¾-in.-wide, ⅜-in.-deep dado that is ¾ in. from the back end of each drawer side. The drawer back panel will fit into these dado grooves. A hold-down attachment on the miter gauge helps secure the workpiece as you cut the dadoes.

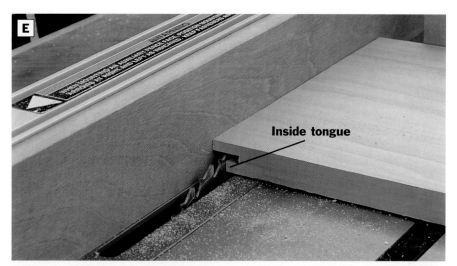

PHOTO E: Complete the locking double-dado joinery in the drawer front panel by trimming ⅜ in. from the inside tongue of the dado groove.

Inside tongue

PHOTO F: Glue the drawer sides, front and back together, clamp up the drawer and check for square. Slide the drawer bottom into the dado and nail the drawer bottom to the drawer back with 1-in. brads.

PHOTO G: Center the drawer face on the drawer front, leaving a ⅜-in. overhang all around the drawer front, and hold the drawer face in place with spring clamps. Fasten the drawer face to the drawer front with two 1¼-in. wood screws.

in. up from the bottom edge of the front panel. Cut the drawer opening with a jig saw, using a straightedge to guide the saw **(See Photo C).** Drill starter holes in the corners of the cutout area to make it easier to turn the jigsaw and start the next cut. Sand the edges of the opening so it's straight and square.

BUILD THE DRAWER

The drawer is fashioned from poplar sides, front and back panels joined with locking double-dado joints at the front. A plywood drawer bottom is fitted into dadoes in the bottoms of the sides and front. A poplar drawer face is attached to the drawer after it is assembled and mounted.

8 Cut the drawer front, sides and back to size.

9 Cut dadoes for the drawer bottom in the drawer sides and drawer front. The dadoes should be ¼ in. wide by ⅜ in. deep. Position the dado grooves ½ in. up from the bottom of each panel. We used a table saw and dado-blade set to make the cuts.

10 Cut a ¼-in-wide by ⅜-in.-deep dado ¼ in. in from the front edge of each drawer side. (This is the first step in constructing the locking double-dado joint that holds the drawer sides to the drawer front.)

11 Cut a ¾-in.-wide × ⅜-in.-deep dado in the back of each drawer side panel, ¾ in. from the face edge, to accept the drawer back panel **(See Photo D).**

12 Cut a ¼ × ¾-in.-deep dado in each end of the drawer front, ¼ in. from the back face. Use a tall auxiliary fence to support the panel as you feed it through the table saw blade.

13 Trim ⅜ in. off the inside tongues of the drawer front to create the shape for the locking double-dado (**See Photo E**) and *Detail: Drawer Joints,* page 127. Dry-fit the sides, front and back of the drawer, and adjust the drawer joints if needed.

14 Cut the drawer bottom to size from ¼-in.-thick plywood.

15 Spread glue into all the dado grooves of the drawer parts except for the drawer bottom dado. Fit the drawer sides into the drawer front, the drawer back into the drawer sides, and slide the drawer bottom into place. Clamp the drawer parts together. Tack the drawer bottom to the drawer back with 1-in. brads driven up through the bottom panel and into the back (**See Photo F**).

16 Cut the drawer face to size. Cut a 20° chamfer on the front outside edges, using a table saw. Finish-sand the drawer face, center it on the drawer front with an even ⅜-in. overhang all around and chamfers facing out, and fasten the drawer face to the drawer front with two #8 × 1¼-in. screws (**See Photo G**).

MOUNT THE DRAWER
We used wood strips to build drawer runners and guides for mounting the drawer in the drawer opening. The runners and guides are fashioned into four pairs and attached at each corner of the opening.

17 Cut the drawer runners and guides to size and join them into four pairs as shown in Photo H and the diagram on page 127. Use

PHOTO H: Screw the two-piece drawer runners to the chest sides, keeping the runners tight against the center shelf (above the drawer) and bottom panel (below the drawer).

Blade guard removed for clarity

PHOTO I: Bevel-cut the top edges of each base piece at 20°.

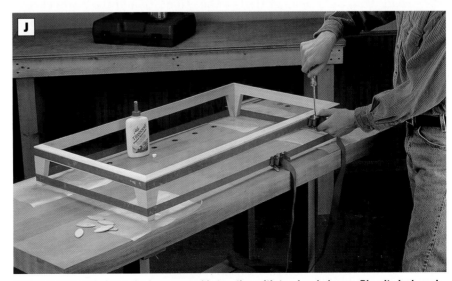

PHOTO J: Glue and clamp the base assembly together with two band clamps. Biscuits lock each corner joint together to help keep the base parts aligned during clamping.

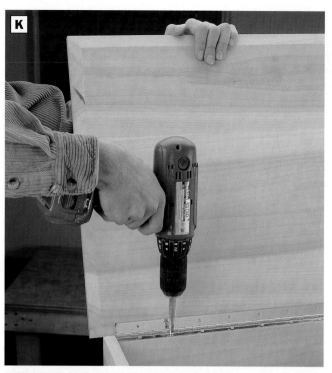

PHOTO K: Install the lid to the carcase back temporarily with the piano hinge and a few screws in each hinge leaf. Be sure the lid-edge bevels face in toward the carcase. Check the fit of the lid on the carcase, then remove the screws and hinge to prepare for finishing the cabinet.

PHOTO L: Prime and paint the outer surfaces of the cabinet including the lid, cabinet back and drawer front. Use an oil-based primer and paint for best results. Those surfaces that will be left natural should be finished with Danish oil or clear varnish.

glue and countersunk #8 × 1¼-in. screws to join the runners and guides together.

⑱ Mount the four drawer runner assemblies to the inside of the chest in the upper and lower corners of the drawer compartment (See *Front Section View,* page 127). Hold them tight against the center shelf or bottom panel, and screw through the guides and into the carcase sides with #8 × 1¾-in. flathead wood screws (**See Photo H).** NOTE: *Be sure the bottom two drawer runners sit even with or slightly above the bottom edge of the drawer cutout so that the drawer will ride on the runners.*

⑲ Test the fit of the drawer by inserting it into the drawer opening. If the front drawer panel extends past the front of the chest, trim the back ends of the drawer sides slightly.

MAKE THE BASE

The base pieces are cut out in the center to create "feet" when the base is assembled (See drawings on pages 126 and 127).

⑳ Cut the base ends and base sides to size. Lay out the feet cutouts in the base parts to keep the orientation of the parts clear. Bevel-miter the ends of each base piece at 45°. Then cut a 20° chamfer along the top edge of each base piece (**See Photo I).**

㉑ Make the feet cutouts in the base side and end pieces with a jig saw or band saw, and sand the cut edges smooth.

㉒ Use a biscuit joiner to cut two #20 biscuit slots along each mitered edge of the four base pieces. The biscuits will help align the base parts during glue-up.

㉓ Spread glue along the mitered

ends of the base pieces and into the biscuit slots, assemble the base parts, and pull the mitered joints tight with strap clamps (**See Photo J).** When the glue dries, remove the clamps.

㉔ Cut the four base cleats to size and fasten them to the inside faces of the base parts with glue and #8 × 1¼-in. flathead wood screws. Align the cleats so the bottom edges of the cleats are flush with the tops of the feet cutouts on the base assembly.

BUILD & ATTACH THE LID

㉕ Rip and edge-joint enough stock to glue up a 18¾-in.-wide by 37½-in.-long panel for the lid. Reinforce the joints between the boards with #20 biscuits. Glue up and clamp the panel.

㉖ Cut a 20° chamfer around the underside of the lid. Since you'll need to stand the lid panel on edge and end to cut the chamfers, use a tall auxiliary fence if you make these cuts on the table saw to help support the workpiece.

27 Temporarily attach the lid to the back panel of the chest with a 34½-in.-long piano hinge and a few hinge screws **(See Photo K).** Make sure the lid overhangs the sides of the chest evenly before you install the hinge screws.

FINISHING TOUCHES

28 Before applying your finish, remove the piano hinge. Make sure all wood is finish-sanded to 150- or 180-grit, then apply primer and paint **(See Photo L).** The inside of the chest and chest bottom, as well as the inside and outside of the drawer parts (except the drawer face), can be finished with a clear topcoat, such as Danish oil or clear varnish. Let the finish dry.

29 Lay the chest upside-down and set the base into position on the carcase so that the base cleats rest on the chest bottom. Attach the base to the chest with countersunk #8 × 1½-in. wood screws driven through the cleats and into the chest **(See Photo M).**

30 Attach the lid to the cabinet with the piano hinge, using ½-in.-long brass wood screws, screwing through every leaf hinge hole **(See Photo N).** Install lid support hardware at this time to hold the lid open or keep the lid from slamming. This hardware is available from most woodworking supply stores and home centers.

31 Finish the drawer knobs with Danish oil or varnish and attach them to the drawer face, centering them vertically on the drawer face and 6 in. in from each end.

PHOTO M: Fit the base over the chest bottom and attach the base with #8 × 1½-in. countersunk wood screws driven through the base cleats and into the chest carcase.

PHOTO N: Reattach the lid to the chest with the piano hinge. Drill a pilot hole for each ½-in. brass screw first, then drive a screw into every hole in both hinge leaves. Install lid support hardware to keep the lid from slamming and to hold it open.

Made-to-order Mailbox

Dress up the entry to your home with this Arts and Crafts-style mailbox. Made from white oak, our mailbox design features grooved veining on the door, as well as door battens clad in copper foil. Functional as well as attractive, the mailbox provides access to its contents through both a hinged lid and front door.

Vital Statistics: Made-to-order Mailbox

TYPE: Mailbox

OVERALL SIZE: 14W by 19H by 6D

MATERIAL: White oak

JOINERY: Biscuit joints, butt joints

CONSTRUCTION DETAILS:

· Solid-wood construction throughout
· Board-and-batten style door
· Mail accessible from both the hinged lid and door
· Door battens wrapped with copper foil to enhance Arts and Crafts-style appearance
· Hidden French cleats for surface mounting

FINISHING OPTIONS: Use an oil-based stain and topcoat followed by three coats of clear exterior-grade polyurethane varnish with UV protectant

Building time

 PREPARING STOCK
1 hour

 LAYOUT
1 hour

 CUTTING PARTS
2 hours

 ASSEMBLY
4 hours

 FINISHING
1-2 hours

TOTAL: 9-10 hours

Tools you'll use

· Jointer
· Planer
· Table saw
· Jig saw, band saw or power miter saw
· Router with 3/16-in. veining (V-groove) bit
· Biscuit joiner
· Bar, pipe, spring clamps
· Aviator snips
· Drill/driver
· Tack hammer
· Screwdriver

HANDYMAN Shopping list

- ☐ (2) 3/4 × 5½ in. × 8 ft. white oak (nominal 1 × 6)
- ☐ (1) 1/64 × 12 × 12 in. copper foil
- ☐ #10 biscuits
- ☐ 12 in. brass piano hinge, screws
- ☐ (2) 1 × 1 in. brass butt hinges, screws
- ☐ 1¼ × 1¼ in. oak door pull
- ☐ Magnetic catch
- ☐ #8 galvanized flathead wood screws (1-, 2-in.)
- ☐ Moisture-resistant wood glue
- ☐ Contact cement
- ☐ ½ in. copper nails
- ☐ Finishing materials

Made-to-order Mailbox

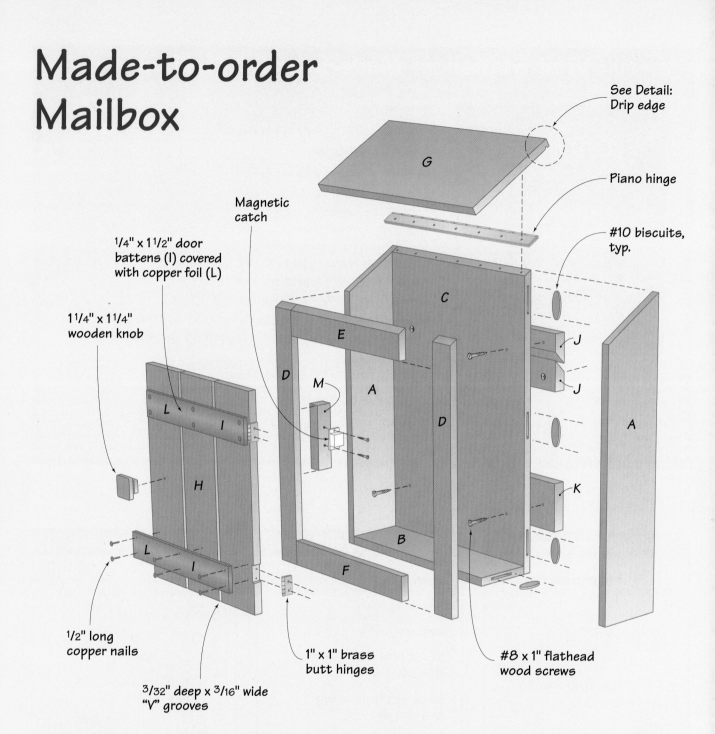

See Detail: Drip edge

Piano hinge

Magnetic catch

1/4" x 1 1/2" door battens (I) covered with copper foil (L)

#10 biscuits, typ.

1 1/4" x 1 1/4" wooden knob

1/2" long copper nails

3/32" deep x 3/16" wide "V" grooves

1" x 1" brass butt hinges

#8 x 1" flathead wood screws

Made-to-order Mailbox Cutting List

Part	No.	Size	Material
A. Sides	2	1/2 × 4 × 18 1/8 in.	White oak
B. Bottom	1	1/2 × 3 1/2 × 12 in.	"
C. Back	1	1/2 × 12 × 18 1/8 in.	"
D. Front stiles	2	1/2 × 1 1/2 × 15 13/16 in.	"
E. Front rail (Upper)	1	1/2 × 1 13/16 × 10 in.	"
F. Front rail (Lower)	1	1/2 × 1 1/2 × 10 in.	"

Part	No.	Size	Material
G. Lid	1	1/2 × 6 1/2 × 14 in.	White oak
H. Door	1	1/2 × 9 7/8 × 12 3/8 in.	"
I. Door battens	2	1/4 × 1 1/2 × 9 3/8 in.	"
J. French cleats	2	3/4 × 1 7/8 × 11 in.	"
K. Spacer cleat	1	3/4 × 3 × 11 in.	"
L. Foil cladding	2	Cut to fit	Copper foil
M. Catch cleat	1	3/4 × 1 × 4 in.	"

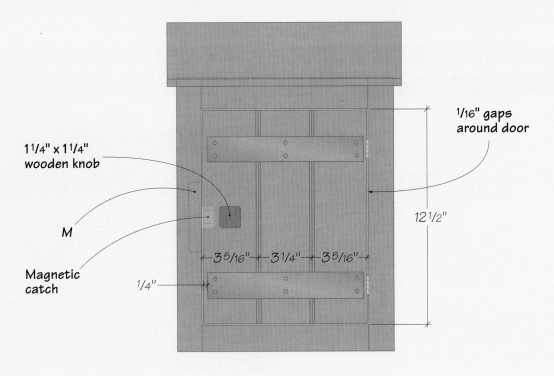

1¼" x 1¼" wooden knob

M

Magnetic catch

1/16" gaps around door

12 1/2"

3 5/16" — 3 1/4" — 3 5/16"

1/4"

FRONT VIEW

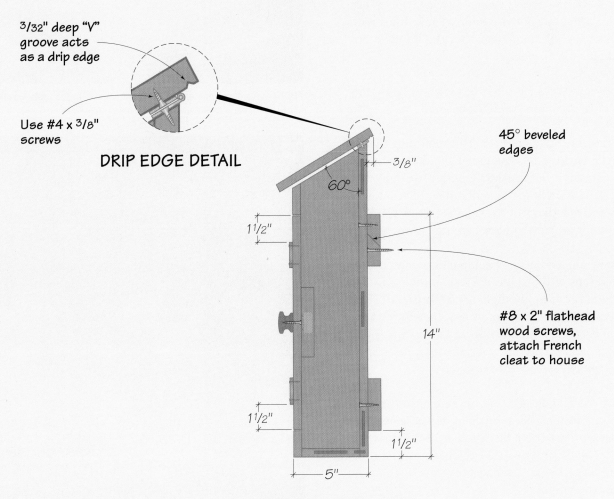

3/32" deep "V" groove acts as a drip edge

Use #4 x 3/8" screws

DRIP EDGE DETAIL

60°

3/8"

45° beveled edges

1 1/2"

14"

#8 x 2" flathead wood screws, attach French cleat to house

1 1/2"

1 1/2"

5"

SIDE SECTION VIEW

ASSEMBLE THE BOX

1 Surface-plane all the ¾-in.-thick stock you plan to use for the mailbox front, back, sides, bottom, lid, door and face frame parts to ½-in. thick. Flatten a long edge of this ½-in.-thick stock on the jointer.

2 Rip- and cross-cut the mailbox side pieces to size. Mark a 30° line across the face of each side piece, starting from one of the corners. These lines will establish the 60° angle tops that the lid rests on. Cut the angles in the sides.

3 Rip- and cross-cut a 3½-in.-wide by 12-in.-long piece of stock for the mailbox bottom.

4 Edge-glue strips of ½-in.-thick oak together to form the back panel. The panel should be at least 1 in. longer than the finished length of 18⅛ in. If you don't mind a little waste, make the glue-up long enough to cut the door as well (See Step 11). When the glue dries, rip the back panel to 12 in. wide.

5 Bevel one end of the back panel to match the beveled tops of the sides. We used a table saw with the blade set at a 30° angle **(See Photo A).** NOTE: *If you've set up your saw accurately, the blade should cut the bevel without shortening the overall length of the back panel. Test the saw setup on a piece of scrap before you cut the actual workpiece.*

6 Lay out and cut #10 biscuit slots into the back, sides and bottom pieces of the mailbox **(See Photo B).** Use at least three biscuits per back joint (See *Side Section View,* page 137). Make sure the top and bottom biscuit slots are no closer than 1 in. to the ends of the panel.

7 Apply moisture-resistant wood glue into the biscuit slots and onto the mating edges of each joint.

Blade guard removed for clarity

PHOTO A: Bevel-cut one end of the back panel with the table saw blade set to 30°, then cross-cut the panel to final length.

PHOTO B: Cut slots for #10 biscuits in the mailbox sides, back and bottom to help align the joints during glue-up. Clamp the workpieces securely to the workbench when you cut the slots.

PHOTO C: Glue and clamp up the sides, back and bottom with moisture-resistant wood glue and biscuits to create the mailbox carcase. Use wood cauls between the clamp jaws and the workpieces to distribute the clamping pressure evenly.

Insert biscuits and clamp the sides, back and bottom together. Wipe away any glue squeeze-out with a damp cloth **(See Photo C).**

ADD THE FACE FRAME

Because the face frame for the mailbox is made with lightweight, ½-in.-thick stock, it can be assembled and attached to the carcase with glue only. If your mailbox will be unprotected from the elements, nail the face frame to the carcase with 1¼-in. galvanized nails to reinforce the joints.

8 Rip- and cross-cut ½-in.-thick stock for the face frame rails and stiles. Glue and clamp the frame together with moisture-resistant wood glue **(See Photo D).**

9 Tilt the table saw blade to 30° and bevel the top edge of the face frame. Take care to ensure that this bevel cut does not shorten the overall length of the face frame.

10 Test the fit of the face frame on the mailbox carcase. Glue and clamp the face frame to the box, aligning the bevel on the face frame with the angled side panels. Clean up excess glue with a wet rag, and finish-sand the exterior of the box when the glue dries.

PHOTO D: Glue and clamp the face frame together. Check the assembly for square by measuring across the diagonals—they should be equal. A bar or pipe clamp can be used to adjust the diagonals and keep the glue-up square.

BUILD THE DOOR & LID

11 Edge-joint and glue up lengths of ½-in.-thick stock to create the door panel.

12 Cut the two V-grooves in the front face of the door. We used a table-mounted router and a ³⁄₁₆-in. veining bit, set to cut to a depth of ³⁄₃₂ in. **(See Photo E).** Adjust the bit height to ³⁄₃₂ in. and set the router table fence 3⁵⁄₁₆ in. from the bit. You could also use a router and straightedge guide to make these V-grooves.

13 Edge-joint and glue up lengths of ½-in. stock to create the lid, and cut to size. Cut a ³⁄₃₂-in.-deep drip edge ¼ in. in from the back edge of the lid, using a veining bit. Finish-sand the lid and the door.

14 Apply your finish of choice to the door. We used oil-based, medium golden oak wood stain and three coats of exterior-grade polyurethane varnish.

15 We attached decorative battens to the front of the door clad with copper foil sheeting to add visual interest. Cut the door battens to size from ¼-in.-thick oak. Lay them on a sheet of copper foil and trace around each batten with a marker. Use aviator snips or scissors to cut out the two copper batten

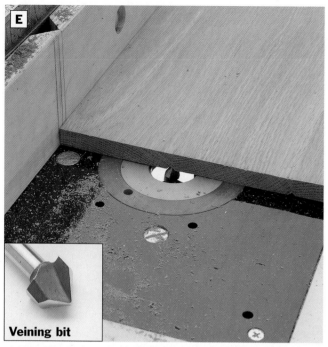

PHOTO E: Cut two V-grooves into the front of the door panel, centered 3⅝16 in. from each edge, using a table-mounted router and 3⁄16-in. veining bit (See inset photo).

Veining bit

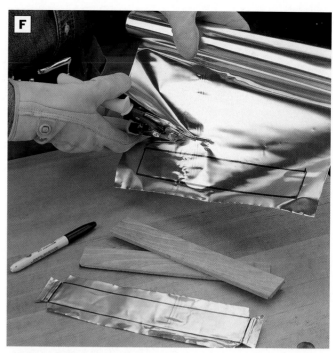

PHOTO F: Outline the wood battens on a sheet of copper foil, then cut along the outlines with an aviator snips. Allow an extra ¾ in. of foil on all sides of each batten.

wraps, allowing an extra ¾ in. of foil around the batten layout lines. Notch out the corners of the foil to help create sharper corners when you wrap each batten **(See Photo F).**

16 Apply contact cement to the face and sides of each batten and to the back of the foil cladding. Center each batten within the layout lines you drew on the foil in Step 15. Fold the ends of the copper around the batten first, then carefully wrap the sides over the ends **(See Photo G).** Smooth the face side of each batten by buffing with a soft cloth before the contact cement cures.

17 Attach the clad battens to the front of the door with glue and ½-in. copper nails driven into pilot holes **(See Photo H).** The battens should be centered side-to-side on the door and spaced 1½-in. from the top and bottom of the door.

HANG THE DOOR & LID

18 Lay out two hinge mortises on the edge of the door and on the inside edge of the face frame stile. The mortises should be aligned with the door battens, and the gap between the door and the upper and lower face frame rail should be equal. Cut the mortises with a sharp chisel, then hang the door. Drill pilot holes for the hinge screws first.

PHOTO G: Clad the batten strips in copper foil bonded with contact cement. Fold the foil ends around the back of each batten, then the edges over the ends. Work carefully to keep the batten corners crisp and the foil smooth.

PHOTO H: Glue and clamp the battens in place on the door front. Reinforce with ½-in. copper nails driven through pilot holes (we used two rows of three nails for each batten).

PHOTO I: Attach the lid to the mailbox with a piano hinge, keeping the drip edge on the lid above the hinge. Drill pilot holes for the brass hinge screws first.

⓳ Glue the catch cleat to the inside of the face frame, then install a magnetic door catch.

⓴ Attach the lid to the mailbox with a piano hinge **(See Photo I).** Position the lid so that the lid ends overhang the box sides evenly and the drip edge groove is behind the piano hinge (See *Drip Edge Detail,* page 137). Attach the wooden doorknob.

ATTACH THE CLEAT & SPACER

㉑ Rip- and cross-cut the French cleats to size. Bevel one edge of each cleat to 45°. Attach one French cleat (bevel side in and facing down) to the mailbox back with glue and 1-in. galvanized screws (See *Side Section View,* page 137). Cut the bottom spacer to size and attach it to the mailbox back with glue and #8 × 1-in. screws.

APPLY FINISH & HANG THE MAILBOX

㉒ Finish the mailbox, including the cleats and spacer, to match the door (you may want to remove the hinges first).

㉓ Attach the other beveled French cleat to the side of the house (bevel side in and facing up) with 2-in. galvanized wood screws. Hang the mailbox on the house cleat so the bevels interlock **(See Photo J).** Drive a 2-in. screw through the spacer and into the house siding to lock the mailbox in place.

PHOTO J: Level and attach a French cleat to the house siding with 2-in. galvanized flathead wood screws. Position the cleat on lap siding so the mailbox's bottom cleat will keep the mailbox plumb with the house. Anchor the mailbox to the house by driving another 2-in. screw through both the back panel and bottom cleat and into the house siding.

Corner Cupboard

T urn an unused corner of your kitchen or dining room into a display area with this reproduction of a Colonial-style corner cupboard. Made from dimensional pine, our cupboard features a contoured face frame, three open shelf areas for display purposes and hangs on the walls by way of hidden French cleats.

Vital Statistics: Corner Cupboard

TYPE: Corner cupboard

OVERALL SIZE: 34W by 42¾H by 13D

MATERIAL: Pine

JOINERY: Biscuit joints on face frame; reinforced butt joints on carcase

CONSTRUCTION DETAILS:
· Curved face frame details accentuate Colonial styling
· Space-saving corner design creates ample display area
· Painted pine makes this an economical project to build
· Cabinet hangs on wall with hidden French cleats

FINISHING OPTIONS: Primer and paint or dark stain with clear topcoat

Building time

PREPARING STOCK
2 hours

LAYOUT
2-4 hours

CUTTING PARTS
2-4 hours

ASSEMBLY
2-3 hours

FINISHING
1-2 hours

TOTAL: 9-15 hours

Tools you'll use

· Jointer
· Table saw
· Power miter saw
· Circular saw with edge guide
· Router with piloted 5⁄32-in. ogee bit, ½-in.-rad. cove bit
· Biscuit joiner
· Bar or pipe clamps
· Jig saw
· Back saw or Japanese-style pull saw
· Hammer and nailset
· Drill/driver
· Drill press drum sander or spindle sander

Shopping list

- [ ] (5) ¾ × 5¼ in. × 10 ft. pine (nominal 1 × 6)
- [ ] (1) ¾ × 9¼ in. × 8 ft. pine (nominal 1 × 10)
- [ ] #20 biscuits
- [ ] Wood glue
- [ ] #8 flathead wood screws (1-, 1½-, 2½-in.)
- [ ] Finish nails (3d, 4d, 6d)
- [ ] Finishing materials
- [ ] Heavy-duty wall anchors and screws

Corner Cupboard

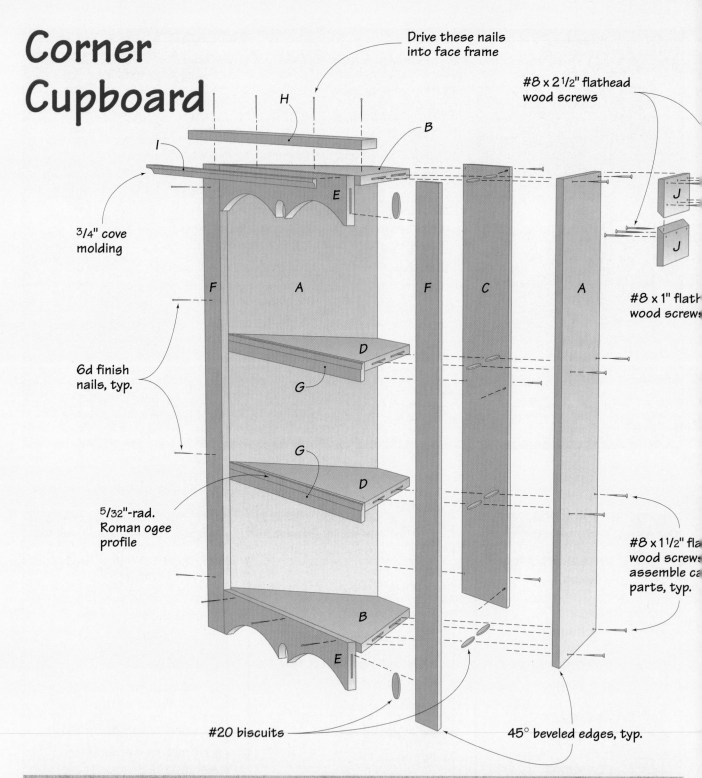

Drive these nails into face frame

#8 x 2½" flathead wood screws

H

B

I

¾" cove molding

E

F

A

F

C

A

J

J

#8 x 1" flath wood screws

D

6d finish nails, typ.

G

G

D

#8 x 1½" fla wood screws assemble ca parts, typ.

5/32"-rad. Roman ogee profile

B

E

#20 biscuits

45° beveled edges, typ.

Corner Cupboard Cutting List

Part	No.	Size	Material		Part	No.	Size	Material
A. Sides	2	¾ × 15⅝ × 38¾ in.	Pine		**F.** Face frame stiles	2	¾ × 3½ × 42 in.	Pine
B. Top, Bottom	2	¾ × 10½ × 27 in.	"		**G.** Shelf edge	2	¾ × 1½ × 27 in.	"
C. Back	1	¾ × 8 × 38¾ in.	"		**H.** Crown	1	¾ × 3 × 34 in.	"
D. Fixed shelves	2	¾ × 9¾ × 25½ in.	"		**I.** Cove molding	1	¾ × ¾ × 34 in.	"
E. Face frame rails	2	¾ × 4 × 25 in.	"		**J.** French cleats	4	½ × 3 × 12 in.	"

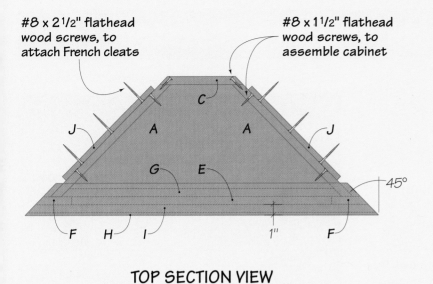

#8 x 2¹/₂" flathead wood screws, to attach French cleats

#8 x 1¹/₂" flathead wood screws, to assemble cabinet

45°

1"

TOP SECTION VIEW

3"

B

10¹/₂"

13¹/₂"

¢

TOP & BOTTOM

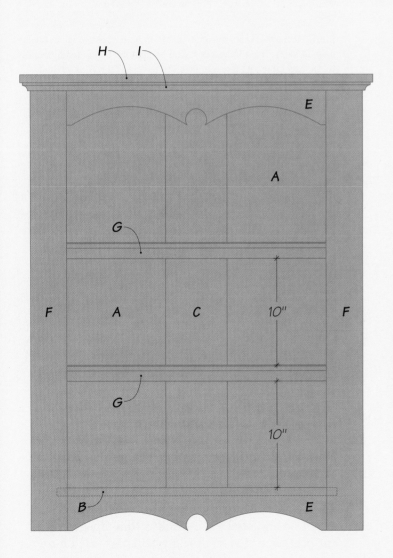

H   I

E

A

G

F   A   C   F

10"

G

10"

B   E

FRONT VIEW

3"

D

9³/₄"

12³/₄"

¢

FIXED SHELVES

Grid squares are 1" x 1"

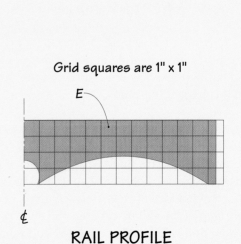

E

¢

RAIL PROFILE

PHOTO A: Bevel-rip the glued-up panels on both edges to make the cabinet sides. The 45° bevels should be parallel. Clamp featherboards to the saw table and fence to hold the panels securely as you cut.

ASSEMBLE THE CARCASE

❶ Edge-glue panels to use for the cabinet sides, top and bottom. We used 1 × 6 pine. Make sure to joint all edges first. The panels should be at least 1 in. longer and wider than the finished sizes of the parts. After the glue has dried, smooth the faces of the panels with a hand plane or cabinet scraper and a random-orbit sander.

❷ Bevel-rip one edge of each carcase side panel at 45°. Then make a parallel bevel cut on the opposite edge to rip the panel to width (**See Photo A**). Cross-cut the sides to length.

❸ Lay out the carcase top, bottom and fixed shelves according to the drawings on page 145. Since the top and bottom of the carcase are the same size, as are the fixed shelves, stack the glued-up panels on top of one another for similar-sized carcase parts, and draw the layout lines on the top panel. Then screw the panels together in the waste areas (away from where the saw blade will run). Use a circular saw and a straightedge cutting guide to gang-cut the angled edges in the workpieces (**See Photo B**). *TIP: You can make an edge guide for your saw by screwing a scrap of edge-jointed 1 × 4 to a strip of ¼-in.-thick hardboard, then running the saw along the 1× to trim the hardboard, creating a blade reference edge.* Align and clamp the cutting guide to one of the ganged stacks and cut both carcase parts at the same time. Then gang-cut the other parts.

❹ Mark the locations for the carcase top and bottom and fixed shelves on the cabinet sides. The carcase top and bottom are flush with the ends of the carcase sides. The fixed shelves are spaced 11½ in. and 23 in. from the top face of the carcase bottom. Make reference marks for #20 biscuits on the shelves, top and bottom and sides, and use four biscuits per joint (**See**

PHOTO B: Gang-cut the carcase top and bottom panels to size, then gang-cut the fixed shelves. Use an edge guide clamped to the workpiece and your workbench to ensure straight cuts.

Photo C). Cut biscuit slots in the mating parts of each joint.

❺ Rip-cut and cross-cut the two shelf edge strips to size. Use a piloted 5⁄32-in.-radius Roman ogee bit to cut profiles in the shelf edge strips. We used a router table to cut the profiles, but a hand-held router would also work (**See Photo D**).

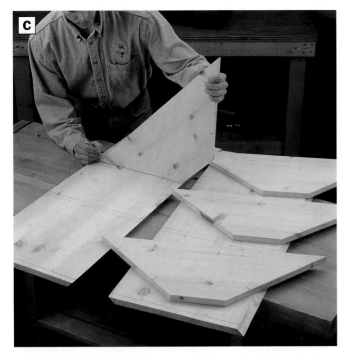

PHOTO C: Lay out all the carcase parts and draw alignment marks for biscuit joints. Be sure to keep the orientation of the side panel bevels in mind when you lay out and mark the parts.

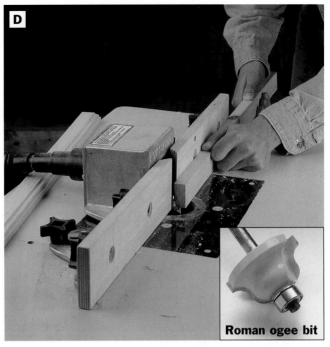

PHOTO D: Rout an ogee profile along one edge of both shelf edge strips with a piloted 5/32-in.-radius Roman ogee bit (See inset). The edging is oversize at this stage to keep your fingers clear of the bit.

6 Glue the shelf edging to the front edges of the fixed shelves so the profiled edge is flush with the top of each shelf. Use masking tape to hold the edging in place while the glue dries. The edging is oversize and should overhang the shelves on both ends. Let the glue dry and remove the tape.

7 Trim the overhanging shelf edging to continue the lines of the angled sides of the shelves, using a back saw or fine-toothed Japanese-style pull saw. Clamp the shelves to your workbench for easier cutting (**See Photo E**). Work carefully to avoid splintering the edges of the edging as you make the cuts.

8 Rip the carcase back to width from 1 × 10 stock, and bevel both long edges at 45° on the table saw. The bevels should face in opposite directions from one another. Then cross-cut the back panel to length.

9 Finish-sand the carcase parts and assemble the carcase with biscuits in place, to check the fit of all the parts. You'll attach the sides to the top, bottom and fixed shelves first, then attach the back to the sides. Drill countersunk pilot holes first, then fasten the carcase parts together using 1½-in. flathead wood screws. Screw the carcase sides to the shelves, then drill angled pilot holes through the back and into the sides, slide the back into place, and attach it with screws (**See Photo F**).

PHOTO E: Clamp the fixed shelves to your workbench and trim the profiled shelf edging to match the angled ends of the shelves. We used a fine-toothed Japanese-style pull saw to make the cuts.

ATTACH THE FACE FRAME

10 Rip- and cross-cut the face frame stiles to size. Bevel one edge of each stile to 45° on the table saw.

11 Rip- and cross-cut the face frame rails to size, according to the *Cutting List,* page 144. Enlarge the grid pattern on page 145 to full size on paper for the rail profile, then glue it to a piece of scrap plywood. Cut the plywood to shape, creating a half template

PHOTO F: Assemble the carcase parts using #8 × 1½-in. flathead wood screws to reinforce the joints. Attach the cupboard back by driving the screws at an angle through the back and into the sides.

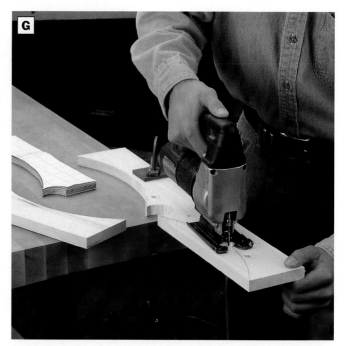

PHOTO G: Make a template of the face-frame rail profile and use it to lay out the curves on the rails. Cut the profiles using a jig saw, band saw or scroll saw.

for the rail profile. Trace the outlines of the template onto a rail, then flip the template over and finish the outline by tracing the mirror image on the rest of the rail. Outline the second rail. Cut out the rail profiles with a jig saw, band saw or scroll saw and smooth the cut edges **(See Photo G)**. *Tip: A drum sander in the drill press or a spindle sander is a great way to smooth up all the curved sawn edges.*

12 Arrange the face frame parts together. The ends of the rails should butt against the flat edges of the stiles; position the beveled edges of the stiles so they taper toward the back of the cupboard. Cut biscuit slots for #20 biscuits to join the ends of the face frame rails to the stiles, one biscuit per joint. Then glue up and clamp the face frame on a flat surface. NOTE: *You may need to fashion notched clamping pads for the clamp jaws so they'll fit over the beveled edges of the stiles, to keep the clamp jaws from marring the stile bevels.*

13 Align the face frame with the front of the carcase so the top edge of the face-frame top rail is even with the top of the carcase and the stiles overhang the carcase sides evenly. Attach the face frame with wood glue and 4d finish nails. Set the nails below the surface of the face frame with a nailset **(See Photo H).** Fill the nail holes with wood putty and finish-sand the face frame smooth with 180-grit sandpaper.

ATTACH THE CROWN ASSEMBLY

14 Cut the crown strip to rough size (about 36 in. long), then miter the ends at 45° to continue the angled lines of the face frame. Use a table saw or a power miter saw to cut the miters in the workpiece. Finish-sand the front edge of the crown, then attach it to the carcase top and face frame with glue and 4d finish nails. The crown should overhang the face-frame top rail by 1 in.

15 Cut a strip of molding to fit the gap between the crown strip and the face frame. We routed a Roman ogee profile into a strip of stock, then ripped the molding to width on the table saw **(See Photo I).** You could use milled cove molding instead. Miter-cut the molding to length, making sure the ends will follow the lines of the crown and the edges of the face frame. Attach with glue and 3d finish nails.

FINISHING TOUCHES

We painted the cabinet front before attaching the French cleats used to hang it. Because pine is a softwood, we primed the surfaces first, then applied two coats of satin paint. (We chose periwinkle blue because it's similar in tone to the blue milk paint often used to finish Colonial-style furnishings).

16 Cut the French cleats to size from scrap pine, and bevel one edge of each cleat to 45°. Glue and screw one cleat to each side of the cabinet along its top edge, so the beveled edges of the cleats face down and in toward the cabinet. Use three #8 × 1-in. flathead wood screws per cleat (See Photo J).

⓱ To hang the cupboard, attach the two remaining French cleats to the two walls bevel-side up so the bevels face the walls. Level the cleats to one another on the walls and space them 7 in. from the corner. Drive #8 × 2½-in. flathead wood screws through the cleats and into the wall, making sure to hit wall studs. Since the cleats will support the full weight of the cupboard and its contents, use wall anchors and appropriate screws if you cannot attach the cleats to wall studs.

⓲ Hang the cupboard on the wall so the French cleats interlock. The cleat bevels will force the cabinet tight against the wall. Tack the cabinet to the wall with one screw through each side and cleat.

PHOTO H: Attach the face frame to the cupboard carcase with glue and 4d finish nails. Drive the nailheads below the face frame surface with a nailset.

Blade guard removed for clarity

PHOTO I: Rip the cove molding for the cupboard crown to width on the table saw. Use a featherboard and pushstick.

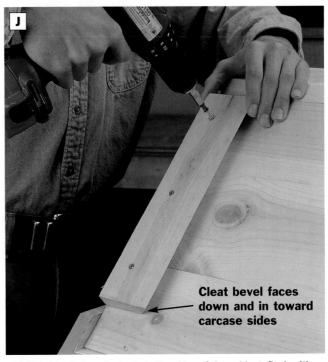

Cleat bevel faces down and in toward carcase sides

PHOTO J: Attach French cleats to the sides of the cabinet, flush with the top of the carcase. The cleat bevels face down and into the sides.

Mission-style Coat Tree

Mission and Arts and Crafts styles are enjoying a resurgence in popularity, mostly because of the simplicity and elegance of these designs. Quartersawn white oak, which was widely used in Mission furniture, is a natural choice for our coat tree. The tapered top and decorative corbels on the feet add to its sleek appearance, which sets it apart from other coat tree styles that can look clumsy and bottom-heavy. We chose to accentuate this traditional reproduction with antique brass-finished coat hooks to give the coat tree a truly vintage look.

Vital Statistics: Mission-style Coat Tree

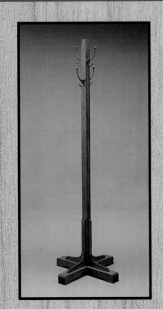

TYPE: Coat tree

OVERALL SIZE: 24W by 24D by 72H

MATERIAL: White oak

JOINERY: Half-lap and butt joints reinforced with screws

CONSTRUCTION DETAILS:
- Tapered and chamfered post top
- Decorative corbels reinforce the post/base connection
- Broad footprint design for stability

FINISHING OPTIONS: Use a medium to dark walnut stain finish for a more traditional wood tone, or topcoat with a clear varnish for a more contemporary look

Building time

PREPARING STOCK
1 hour

LAYOUT
2 hours

CUTTING PARTS
4 hours

ASSEMBLY
2-4 hours

FINISHING
1-2 hours

TOTAL: 10-13 hours

Tools you'll use

- Table saw with dado-blade set
- Jig saw or band saw
- Router with ¾-in. roundover bit
- Belt sander
- Drill/driver
- Spindle sander
- Pipe clamps
- Large spring clamps
- Mallet
- Vix bit

Shopping list

- ☐ (1) 8/4 × 5½ in. × 10 ft. white oak
- ☐ (1) ¾ × 8 in. × 3 ft. white oak
- ☐ #8 flathead wood screws (1½-, 3½-in.)
- ☐ 4d finish nails
- ☐ Wood glue
- ☐ ⅜-in.-dia. oak dowel
- ☐ Finishing materials
- ☐ (4) Brass coat hooks

Mission-style Coat Tree

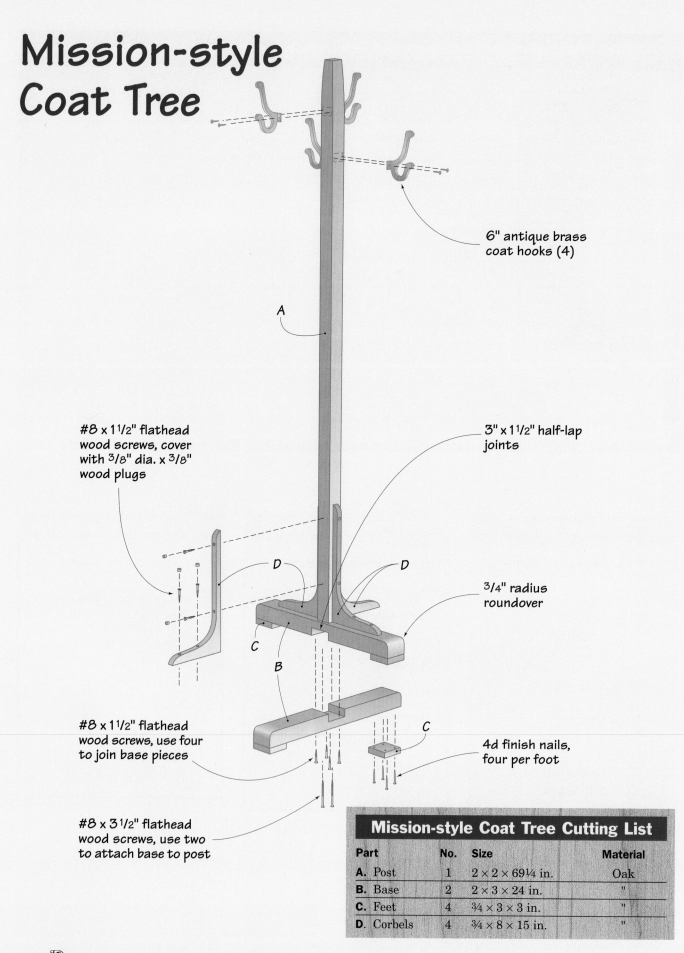

6" antique brass coat hooks (4)

A

#8 x 1¹/2" flathead wood screws, cover with ³/8" dia. x ³/8" wood plugs

3" x 1¹/2" half-lap joints

D

D

³/4" radius roundover

C

B

C

#8 x 1¹/2" flathead wood screws, use four to join base pieces

4d finish nails, four per foot

#8 x 3¹/2" flathead wood screws, use two to attach base to post

Mission-style Coat Tree Cutting List

Part	No.	Size	Material
A. Post	1	2 × 2 × 69¼ in.	Oak
B. Base	2	2 × 3 × 24 in.	"
C. Feet	4	¾ × 3 × 3 in.	"
D. Corbels	4	¾ × 8 × 15 in.	"

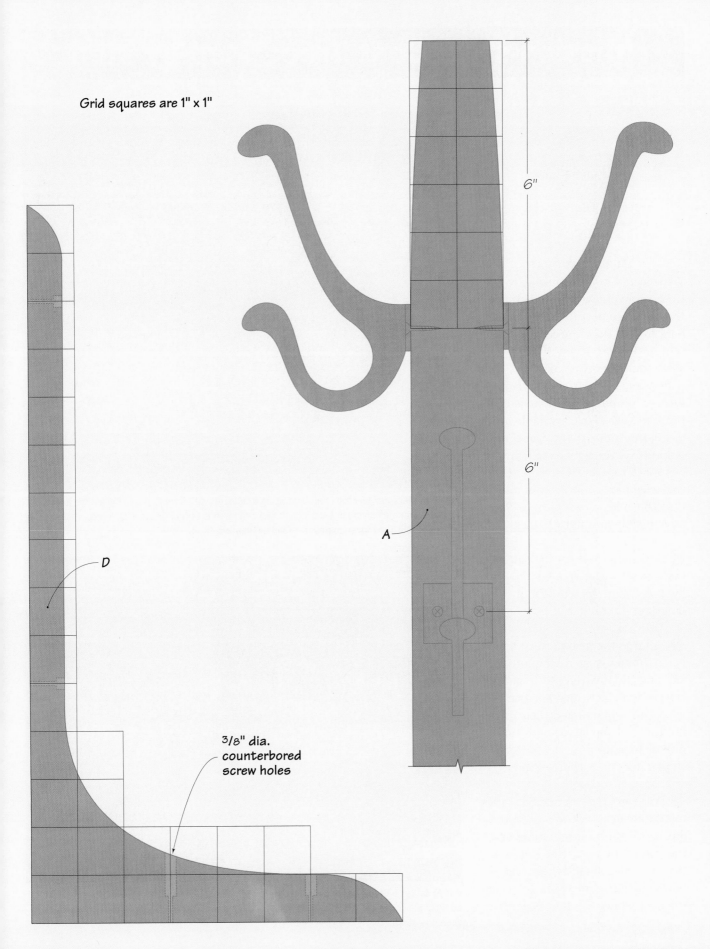

Grid squares are 1" x 1"

6"

6"

A

D

3/8" dia.
counterbored
screw holes

BUILD THE POST

We selected a piece of solid ¾-thick quartersawn white oak for the coat tree post and base members to give these pieces a consistent grain pattern on all four sides (quartersawn oak was widely used for Mission-style furniture). If quartersawn stock of this thickness isn't available at your local lumberyard, you could laminate several pieces of thinner oak stock together to create the coat tree parts, but keep in mind that the sides of the parts will have visible lamination lines.

❶ Edge-joint and rip the oak stock for the coat tree post to 2 in. by 2 in. Then crosscut it to a length of 69¼ in.

❷ Enlarge the grid pattern on page 153 to use as a template for shaping the tapered post top. This can be done by drawing a grid with 1-in. squares and then tracing the post top shape onto your grid or by enlarging the pattern shown here on a photocopier.

❸ Transfer the grid pattern taper to all four faces of the post top and mark the square outline on the end of the post where all four tapered sides should meet. Also mark the base line on each face of the post where the taper begins.

Taper base line

PHOTO A: Mark the post top taper lines using a full-size grid pattern, then belt-sand the post top to shape with a medium-grit sanding belt. You may need to redraw lines on each face after sanding it to reestablish the taper contour for sanding adjacent faces.

PHOTO B: Cut half-lap joints into the centers of the base pieces with a dado-blade set. Make multiple passes to cut the 3-in.-wide dadoes, using a miter gauge with a hold-down clamp to guide the stock.

4 Shape the tapers using a belt sander and medium-grit sanding belt, starting at the base line of each taper and working toward the post end **(See Photo A).** Form the tapered profile one side at a time, checking your layout lines frequently. Keep your grid template handy—you'll need to redraw your layout lines in order to shape each adjacent face of the post as you go.

CONSTRUCT THE BASE

5 Rip-cut the two coat tree base pieces from ¾ oak stock and cross-cut them each to 24 in. long.

6 Mark a 3-in.-wide by 1-in.-deep dado, centered across the face of each base member. Once cut, these dadoes will interlock and create a half-lap joint. Install a dado-blade set in your table saw. Set the cutter width to ¾ in. or more and height to 1 in. Cut the dadoes in several passes **(See Photo B).** Test the fit of the half-lap joint; the dadoes should fully interlock. NOTE: *If you don't have a dado-blade set, you could also cut these dadoes with a router and straight bit, guiding the router along a straightedge clamped to the workpiece. If you use this method, plow out the dadoes in several passes of increasing depth until you reach the final 1 in. depth. Otherwise, you could overheat or even break your bit. A set of mortising chisels will also do the trick.*

7 Designate a top and bottom base member (once assembled, the dado will face down on the top base member and up on the bottom base member). Set the two base members side by side and clamp them between two pieces of scrap that are the same height and length as the bases. Install a

PHOTO C: Gang-rout roundovers on the ends of the base members. We used a ¾-in.-roundover bit (See inset photo). Clamp scrap boards of the same height and length outside the base members to prevent the router bit from chipping or following the corners.

PHOTO D: Attach the post to the base with glue and two counterbored #8 × 3½-in. flathead wood screws. Secure the base in your bench vise with the post centered on the base. Make sure the post is centered on the middle of the base assembly.

PHOTO E: After sawing the corbels to rough shape with a jig saw or band saw, smooth the edges and refine the shape. An oscillating spindle sander makes this task quick and easy.

Corbels

PHOTO F: Attach the corbels to the post with glue and #8 × 1½-in. flathead screws, driven into counterbored pilot holes.

¾-in. roundover bit in your router and rout across the top corners of the base and scrap assembly **(See Photo C).** The scrap pieces will keep the router bit from chipping the corners of the base members.

8 Cut four 3 × 3-in. coat tree feet from ¾-in.-thick oak stock. Use glue and four 4d finish nails per foot to attach the feet to the bottom ends of the base pieces. Tip: *Drill a pilot hole for the nails first with a ¹⁄₁₆-in. drill bit. Doing so will help sink the nails more easily into the hard oak.* Set the nailheads below the surface with a nailset, to keep the feet from scratching floors or snagging carpet later on.

ATTACH THE POST TO THE BASE
9 Apply glue to the half-laps of the base members and fasten the base together using four #8 × 1½-in. flathead screws. Drill counterbored pilot holes before you drive in the screws.

10 Set the post onto the base assembly so it is centered and the faces are parallel to the edges of the base members. Drill two countersunk pilot holes up

through the base and into the post. Attach the post with glue and 3½-in. wood screws **(See Photo D).**

BUILD THE CORBELS
The corbels add lateral stability to the coat tree post and give the coat tree some decorative flair. Without them, the weight of coats on the tree could pull the post loose from the base.

11 Cut blanks out of ¾-in.-thick oak stock for the four corbels. Transfer the corbel grid pattern drawing on page 153 to one of the blanks.

12 Cut out the corbel along the waste side of the cutting line with a band saw or jig saw, and smooth the cut edges. We used an oscillating spindle sander **(See Photo E),** but a flexible sanding pad, cabinet scraper or file would also do the trick.

13 Use the finished corbel as a pattern for tracing cutting lines on the three remaining blanks. Follow the same procedure for cutting and sanding the corbels to produce four identical parts.

⑭ Draw reference lines along the centers of the base members and along each face of the post. Center a corbel along the reference lines for each side of the coat tree and clamp them in place. Drill four counterbored pilot holes in each corbel, according to the locations shown on the pattern on page 153. Remove the clamps, apply glue to the corbels, and screw them in place with #8 × 1½-in. flathead wood screws **(See Photo F).**

FINISHING TOUCHES

⑮ Plug the counterbore holes in the corbels with ⅜-in.-dia. white oak plugs. NOTE: *You may want to make your own plugs on the drill press with a plug cutter in scrap white oak stock, since white oak plugs may be difficult to find. Cut the plugs from face grain, rather than end grain, to help hide the plugs. Or you could cut the plugs from walnut, for a contrasting appearance. Walnut was often used to conceal screws in Mission furniture.* Cut the plugs ¼ in. or so longer than necessary. Apply glue to the holes and the plugs, and tap the plugs in with a mallet. When the glue has dried, trim the plugs flush with a flexible Japanese hand saw or tenoning saw, then sand the plug ends smooth.

⑯ Ease all sharp edges of the coat tree, and finish-sand the wood with progressively finer sandpaper, up to 180-grit.

⑰ Apply the stain and protective coating of your choice according to the instructions on the container. We brushed on a walnut oil stain, let it dry, then followed with three coats of satin, oil-based polyurethane varnish **(See Photo G).** It's a good idea to rub between coats of varnish with 0000-grade steel wool to ensure a smooth finish.

⑱ Install the coat hooks in pairs on opposing faces of the post at 6 in., then 12 in. from the post top **(See Photo H).** We chose hooks with an antique finish to enhance the coat tree's vintage styling. *TIP: Use a vix bit for drilling perfectly centered holes for screws used in hinges and other metal hardware, like these coat tree hooks. A guide centers the bit over the screw area. Plunge the bit forward and the spring-loaded drill bit inside drills the hole. The bit then retracts up and out of the way.*

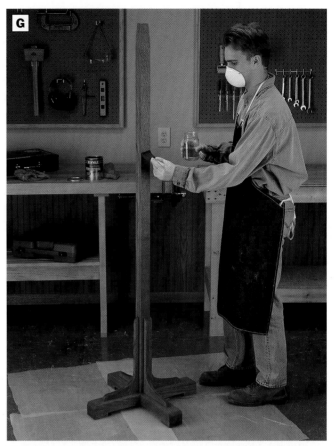

PHOTO G: We used a brush-on walnut oil stain to tint the oak, then topcoated with three coats of satin, oil-based polyurethane varnish.

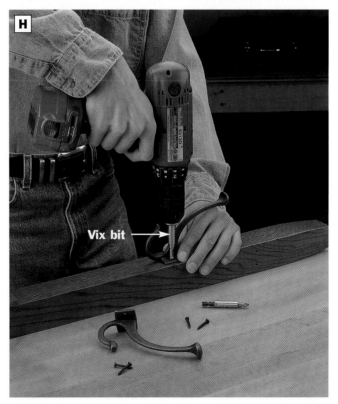

Vix bit

PHOTO H: Use a vix bit to drill holes that are perfectly aligned with the guide holes in the hooks.

Index

Index of Projects